Elijah Middlebrook Haines

**Parliamentary Law**

Elijah Middlebrook Haines

**Parliamentary Law**

ISBN/EAN: 9783337155834

Printed in Europe, USA, Canada, Australia, Japan

Cover: Foto ©Suzi / pixelio.de

More available books at **www.hansebooks.com**

OR,

# RULES OF ORDER

FOR

DELIBERATIVE ASSEMBLIES.

---

— BY —

ELIJAH M. HAINES,

*Ex-Speaker of the House of Representatives of the Illinois General Assembly.*

CHICAGO
THE LEGAL ADVISER PUBLISHING
1885.

# PREFACE.

There is no subject to which we have occasion to resort so much, that is apparently so little understood, as the rules of Parliamentary law. Deliberative assemblies, wherein the application of these rules are required, are a matter of daily occurrence in the country everywhere, not only in official bodies, such as legislative assemblies and city and town councils in municipal corporations, but in public meetings of the people, church meetings, meetings of societies, and the like; and yet it is doubtful if one in ten of the persons who are called upon to preside at such meetings, have ever given the subject of Parliamentary law, or rules of order, that apply on such occasions, a moment's investigation through what has been written and published on the subject. Whatever knowledge they possess, if any, concerning these rules, they have derived from observation while present or in participating in the proceedings of such assemblies.

But the knowledge and experience of a presiding officer in this regard is comparatively of little avail, where there is an absence of knowledge on the subject among those who compose the assembly.

It is not an uncommon thing in a legislative assembly to hear complaints among members of the erroneous or "arbitrary ruling" of the presiding officer. As a general thing, it will be found that such complaints come from those members least acquainted with the rules of parliamentary law. Indeed, a good parliamentarian is not apt to indulge in anything of the kind. He knows that under these rules the presiding officer is constantly subject to the control of the assembly, and that he can make no ruling but what it is at once subject to review and correction if erroneous, on appeal to the assembly.

Where a member is heard urging his grievances on account of some "arbitrary ruling" of the presiding officer, one of two things may be set down as true; either that the member is ignorant of the rules of parliamentary law, or else he has not the ability to avail himself of the remedy which these rules afford him. In general the former reason will be found to be the more correct one to be assigned in his case.

A member may with some propriety complain of the unjust decision of the assembly itself, when appealed to for its decision, because this is final and binding on all; but the ruling of the presiding officer is merely temporary and subject to immediate reversal by the assembly itself. It is true, the assembly may make special rules whereby much power may be vested in the presiding officer; but in the absence of such rules the presiding officer, as before suggested, possesses little or no power whatever; certainly none whereby the rights of members can be in the least prejudiced by the ruling of the presiding officer, for the remedy by appeal is at hand.

The following pages have been prepared as the result of much investigation into the subject embraced, as well as considerable experience as a member of legislative assemblies, including that of presiding officer. The aim has been, especially in presenting those rules which are of most common occurrence and most important in proceedings in deliberative assemblies, to state the same in as brief and concise form as possible, divested of unnecessary verbiage or lengthy illustrations, so that the gist of the rule may be more easily retained in the mind. Every person who desires to become proficient in parliamentary practice, should commit to memory all the most important rules, or those of most common occurrence, especially those which relate to the different kinds of motions, their classification and the order in which they stand.

In England this subject has received the attention of many writers of much experience concerning it, dating from an early period. In this country, the first to give the subject of parliamentary law attention was Thomas Jefferson, who had been Vice President, and presiding officer of the United States Senate, and for a long time Jefferson's manual of parliamentary law and practice was the only book on that subject in use in this country, which was generally adopted in legislative assemblies as the standard of authority. After which Mr. Cushing's excellent manual appeared, which in a great measure superceded that of Mr. Jefferson. At this day there are several works on the subject in use in this country, claiming public favor, so that books on parliamentary law are everywhere at hand; from which it would seem that there is no excuse for this general want of knowledge on this important subject, which is admitted to exist.

ELIJAH M. HAINES.

CHICAGO, January 1, 1884.

# CONTENTS.

|  | PAGE. |
|---|---|
| British Parliament | 11 |
| Origin and Uses of Parliamentary Law | 21 |
| Deliberative Assemblies | 22 |
| The Presiding Officer | 27 |
| The Recording Officer | 31 |
| Public Meetings | 33 |
| Organization of Public Meetings | 35 |
| Manner of Presenting Business | 41 |
| Motions and Manner of Proceeding | 42 |
| Motions in General | 47 |
|     The Previous Question | 48 |
|     Indefinite Postponement | 50 |
|     Motion to Postpone or Lay on the Table | 50 |
|     Motion to Commit | 52 |
| Motion to Amend | 53 |
|     1. Filling Blanks | 53 |
|     2. Striking Out | 55 |
|     3. Amendment by Inserting | 55 |
|     4. Striking Out and Inserting | 56 |
|     5. Division of Proposition | 56 |
|     6. Amendment to an Amendment | 59 |
| The Order and Succession of Questions | 59 |
|     1. Privileged Questions | 60 |
|     2. Incidental Questions | 61 |
|     3. Subsidiary Questions | 62 |

|  | PAGE. |
|---|---|
| Of Reconderation | 65 |
| Of Committees | 68 |
| Committee of the Whole | 73 |
| Appeals | 82 |
| Of Debate | 83 |
| Questions Not Debatable | 92 |
| "Casting Vote" | 95 |
| "Enacting Clause" | 96 |
| Use of the Gavel | 101 |
| Deportment of Members | 106 |
| Peculiarities of Legislation in Parliament | 110 |
| Language of Parliamentary Law | 112 |
| Parliamentary Law in Secret Societies | 115 |
| Summary of General Rules | 121 |
| Index | 155 |

# BRITISH PARLIAMENT.

It is remarked in the following pages of this book that parliamentary law is so called from the rules of order existing from long established usage in the parliament of England.

In this connection a brief history of this parliament, it is believed, would be of practical benefit. It seems that this body originally consisted of that branch of parliament at the present day known as the House of Lords or Peers, meaning the same thing, and at this day the House of Lords is the second of the three bodies which together are said to compose the British legislature, viz: King or Queen, Lords and Commons.

The origin of the House of Lords, which is the origin of the British parliament, is involved in obscurity, and is a body which must be regarded as the natural development of the state of things existing under the Feudal System, when the king ranked as the first among his peers or equals, namely, the nobles who held their lands of the crown by the tenure of military service. It was the tenure of certain lands which constituted a Noble of the Realm in the centuries immediately succeeding the Norman Conquest. The House of Lords, however, is of even older date than this, and has been traced by antiquarians and historians to the very earliest foundations of the British constitution, which were laid in the old Saxon times.

It is, in fact, the great council of the early English chroniclers. It is clear from the historical records of those countries that under the Saxon kings, the Thanes or Nobles, together with the bishops, were the chief advisers of the king, constituting a body not unlike the privy council of the present day. To these in succeeding centuries as the wealth, education and intelligence of the nation increased, were added the representatives of the counties, cities and boroughs of England; and it was not until about the reign of Edward I, that the latter body seems to have become a distinct assembly, and to have been termed the House of Commons, or the Lower House of Parliament. Some historians, indeed, as Elsynge, assert that "the Commons ever held a place for the consultation apart from the Lords;" but this statement is distinctly denied by Sir Edward Coke, who states that he had seen a record, dated in the 30th year of King Henry II, A. D. 1130, of their degrees and seats as one body, and affirms that the separation took place at the desire of the Commons.

From that time to the present day, it seems, no very material change has taken place in the constitution of the Upper House of Parliament, otherwise known as the House of Lords. Since the House of Lords, in conjunction with the sovereign and the House of Commons, composes the supreme legislative body of Great Britain, the consent of each of these three bodies is required in order to give to any resolution the force of law. The voice of the majority in either house binds the whole.

In addition, however, to its legislative functions, the House of Lords possesses judicial authority in virtue of which it exercises the ultimate jurisdiction in matters of appeal from the supreme courts of Great Britain and Ireland. It also has the privilege of trying criminal cases on impeachment by the House of Commons, and also its own members on indictments found against them by the grand jury. In the discharge of these duties the house has the power of requiring the attendance of the judges and the law officers of the crown to assist its decisions with their legal counsel. It is right here to notice a few points in which the House of Lords differs from the Lower House of Parliament. The Lord Chancellor for the time being sits in the Upper House as speaker. When the sovereign goes to open, prorogue or dissolve parliament, he takes his seat upon the royal throne, and the Commons are summoned into his presence, there to receive the communication of his royal will and pleasure. All bills which in any way affect the dignities of the peerage must originate in the upper house. Each member of the House of Lords has the right of voting by proxy upon all measures except in committee; the bearer of the proxy being, of course, some other member of the house. Peers have also the privilege of entering upon the journals of the house their dissent from any measure which has received the sanction of the majority, together with their reasons for dissenting. This is called their protest.

The House of Lords is frequently divided into the Spiritual and Temporal Peers; the latter being again distinguished according to their rank by the titles of Duke, Marquis, Earl, Viscount and Baron. Of the Spiritual Peers, Archbishops take precedence of all Dukes except those of the Blood Royal; while Bishops rank next above Barons. The military titles of Duke (*Dux*) and Marquis (*Marchio, Marchgrave* or *Margrave,* as the governors of marches or frontier provinces were termed,) are derived from the dignities which existed many centuries ago in the Western Empire; while those of Earl (*Eorl* or

*Ealderman*) and Baron are of genuine Saxon origin. The former of these has been identified with the Count (*Comes*) of Western Europe.

The title of Viscount, which originally signified the Count's deputy, was first made a degree of honor in the reign of Henry VI.

The peerage of Great Britain and Ireland admits also of the following classification: 1st. Peers of England; i. e., those whose titles bear date anterior to the union with Scotland in 1707. 2nd. Peers of Scotland; i e., those enjoying the peerage in that country before its union with England 3rd. Peers of Ireland; i. e., created before the union in the year 1800. 4th. Peers of Great Britain; i. e., those created between the years 1707 and 1800. 5th. Peers of the United Kingdom; i. e., those created since the union of the three kingdoms. And 6th, those of the Episcopal Bench, consisting of the two Archbishops and twenty-four English and Welsh Bishops, and one Archbishop and three Bishops of Ireland in annual rotation. Previous to the Reformation, the Spiritual Peers consisted of two Priors and twenty-seven Abbots, in addition to the bishops who at that time considerably outnumbered the Temporal Peers.

The Spiritual Peers consist of all English and Welsh Bishops with the exception of the junior bishop for the time being. The bishops of London and Durham, by virtue of a statute passed 31, Henry VIII and the Bishop of Winchester as Prelate of the Order of the Garter, rank before all other bishops. The Bishop of Meath takes precedence of the other Irish bishops, who follow in the order of their consecration.

The Bishop of Sodor and Man ranks next, and has a seat, but no vote, in the Upper House. In the House of Lords all Peers of England have seats and votes; so have those of Great Britain and the United Kingdom, though the locality from which their title is taken may be either Irish or Scotch. It also frequently happens that Peers of England or of the United Kingdoms hold a superior rank in the Peerages of Scotland or Ireland; in which case, though popularly known by the higher dignity, they still sit and vote in the house by their inferior rank. The Peers of Scotland and Ireland have a place in the house only for their representatives, of which Ireland sends twenty-eight and Scotland sixteen. The Scotch representative peers are chosen with every new parliament; the Irish representative peers are elected for life. Peers of Scotland are no longer created; but on the extinction of three Irish peerages, the Queen has the power to create a new one, which is to rank among the English titles according to the date of its creation.

By the act of union no peer enjoying a British dignity can be elected a representative peer for Ireland; but in the case of a representative peer being elevated to that of the United Kingdom, no vacancy is caused thereby. Scotch peers take precedence of British peers of the same rank created since the union with Scotland; and Irish Peers created before the union with Ireland in like manner take precedence of

British peers created since. Irish peers of later creation than the union rank according to the dates of the patent among the peers of the United Kingdom of Great Britain and Ireland.

It should be observed that the House of Peers, properly speaking, consists only of such members of peerage as otherwise having a right to sit in the house, are neither minors nor insane.*

* Walford's Peerage, 1864.

# PARLIAMENTARY LAW.

### Origin and Uses of Parliamentary Law.

Parliamentary Law consists of rules which are recognized as governing proceedings in deliberative assemblies. It is so called from the rules of order existing from long established usage in the Parliament of England. The Legislative Assemblies of the several States, and the legislative branch of the general government of the United States, being formed upon the principle of the English Parliament, have adopted the like rules for their government, and by general custom in this country, these rules are recognized in all deliberative assemblies. Legislative assemblies, however, for the purpose of certainty, generally adopt by express vote, the rules of parliamentary law, as expounded by some particular writer on the subject, qualified or changed, as circumstances may demand, by various prescribed rules of their own.

## Deliberative Assemblies.

A deliberative assembly is a congregation or convention of persons for the consideration of matters in which all are concerned. The word *assembly*, in this connection, is of itself suggestive of a meeting or congregation of persons considerable in numbers. Where but a few persons come together for any given purpose, their meeting is not strictly in the nature of things a deliberative assembly. The same rules would not necessarily be required in conducting proceedings in the latter case that would be demanded in a deliberative assembly or meeting composed of a large number of persons. For instance, a small number of persons, constituting in the nature of their undertaking a mere executive board, would require but a simple code of rules for their government and action, which would in the order of things scarcely partake of the nature of those established rules of Parliamentary law, which experience has found necessary to be adopted for the government of larger bodies.

So that wherever there is a deliberative assembly convened, or a meeting of persons constituted of numbers sufficient to be deemed a deliberative assembly, the general rules of parliamentary law are applicable at once, as a matter of course, whereby to govern its conduct and regulate its proceedings. These assemblies may be: first, an assemblage of the people themselves; or second, a meeting of a limited or select number of citizens or persons acting in their own behalf.

The former would be a mass meeting of the people without distinction. The latter would be a meeting of citizens of a ward or district, or the members of some particular society or the like.

On the subject of the importance of rules for the government of deliberative assemblies, Mr. Jefferson, in his excellent manual of Parliamentary practice, refers to the remark of Mr. Onslow, whom he styles the ablest among the Speakers of the House of Commons, that "It was a maxim he had often heard when he was a young man, from old and experienced members, that nothing tended more to throw power into the hands of administration and those who acted with the majority of the House of Commons, than a neglect of, or departure from, the rules of proceeding; that these forms, as instituted by our ancestors, operated as a check and control on the actions of the majority; and that they were in many instances a shelter and protection to the minority against the attempts of power."

So far, says Mr. Jefferson, the maxim is certainly true, and is founded in good sense, and he further remarks, citing from Mr. Hatsell, an English writer of distinction on parliamentary law and practice, that it is always in the power of the majority, by their numbers, to stop any improper measures proposed on the part of their opponents; the only weapons by which the minority can defend themselves against similar attempts from those in power, are the forms and rules of proceeding which have been adopted as they were found necessary from time to time and are become the law of the house; by a strict adherence to which the weaker party can only be protected from those irregularities and abuses which these forms were intended to check, and which the wantonness of power is but too often apt to suggest to large and successful majorities. And whether these forms be in all cases the most rational or not, is really not of so great importance. It is much more material that there should be a rule to go by, than what that rule is; that there may be a uniformity of proceeding in business not subject to the caprice of the Speaker, or captiousness of the members. It is very material that order, decency and regularity be preserved in a dignified public body.

We are told by lawyers that courts or judicial tribunals under our system are marked by three constituent parts, the *actor, reus* and *judex.*\* So there are certain essentials which mark or are necessary in every deliberative assembly. In all such bodies there must be a chairman or presiding officer, and a secretary or recording officer. Other officers may be added as may be deemed necessary or the occasion may demand. The organization of a deliberative assembly consists in the election of officers. It cannot be said to be organized until officers are chosen and installed to assist in conducting its proceedings.

Thus the officers of a deliberative assembly may be classified under two different heads or departments, the executive to which the presiding officer belongs, and the recording department to which the clerk or secretary is assigned. In addition to the presiding officer in that department there may be one or more vice-presidents, a sergeant-at-arms or door-keeper, and other officers and assistants as may be deemed necessary, and there may be such assistant clerks and secretaries under that department as may be deemed necessary.

---

\* 3 Blackstone's Commentaries, 25.

## The Presiding Officer.

The general duties of the presiding officer of a deliberative assembly in the absence of any rule of the assembly to the contrary may be summed up as follows :

To open the sessions or sittings of the assembly at the time to which it adjourned by taking the chair and calling the members to order promptly at the time fixed.

To announce the business before the assembly in the order in which it is to be acted upon.

To receive and submit in the proper manner all motions and propositions offered by individual members.

To put to vote all questions which are regularly moved or necessarily arise in the course of the proceedings and to announce the result.

To name which of two or more members who arise at the same time are entitled to address the chair in debate or for purposes of a motion.

To restrain the members when engaged in debate within the rules of order and to enforce the observance of order among the members to the extent of his authority.\*

To receive all messages and other communications and announce the same to the assembly.

To authenticate by his signature when necessary all the acts, orders and proceedings of the assembly.

To inform the assembly or express his opinion when necessary or when referred to for the purpose on a point of order or practice, which may be brought in question

---

\* There is nothing in the rules of parliamentary law giving the presiding officer of a deliberative assembly any power or authority over the conduct of the members in violating the rules of order beyond that of calling attention to the fact that the rules have been disregarded and request that they keep within the rules. If members disregard this request, the most the presiding officer can do in the absence of some fixed rule of the assembly on the subject is to call the attention of the assembly to the conduct complained of and ask what action is desired to be taken.

If the assembly itself declines to interfere, the presiding officer is powerless further in the matter, so far as the naked rules of parliamentary law are concerned. It has been customary for presiding officers to command members for alleged breach of order in debate to resume their seats. The presiding officer has no power to enforce such command unless specially given him by the rules of the assembly.

To name the members who are to serve on committees of the assembly, when not otherwise provided by special rule; and in general—

To represent and stand for the assembly.

When the presiding officer desires or is called upon to read anything for the information of the assembly, or states a motion, he may do so while sitting, but he should rise to put a motion to vote.

In conducting proceedings in deliberative assemblies, much depends upon the presiding officer. The despatch of business depends upon the readiness with which he discharges his duties. Business will be delayed in proportion to his want of promptness in this regard. As soon as a motion or proposition is offered he should proceed at once without hesitation or delay and state it to the assembly in a full and clear voice. If no one rises to speak to it, he should proceed just as promptly to put the motion. He should bear in mind that it is no part of his duty to invite debate.

The presiding officer of a deliberative

assembly is styled *President* or *Chairman*, according to circumstances. There are some religious denominations who in their church meetings in the transaction of business style their presiding officer *Moderator*. From this latter instance is borrowed the style of the presiding officer at town meetings under the New England system.

In the House of Representatives in Congress, and in the popular branch of the legislative assemblies of the several States of the Union, the presiding officer is styled *Speaker*.*

---

* The title *Speaker* is borrowed from that given to the presiding officer of the House of Commons in the British Parliament, having its origin many centuries ago in the obscure past. When the Barons and Burgesses of the Realm, otherwise called the *Commons*, were summoned to parliament, they chose one of their number to be their Speaker, whose duty it was to hear their requests and go before the King and speak for them and in their behalf concerning what they desired. In the reign of Queen Elizabeth, Sir Edward Coke was chosen Speaker of the Commons. In closing his speech to the Queen he said, "I am to make your majesty three petitions in the name of the Commons." Here follow the petitions. See Gurdon's Hist. of Parliament.

Whenever the King desired to communicate anything to the Commons, the custom was to summon their Speaker before him and make the same known to him, who thereupon conveyed it to the Commons.—Ibid.

## The Recording Officer.

The recording officer of the assembly is usually elected by the members in the same manner as the president or presiding officer. He is usually styled *Secretary* or *Clerk* as the assembly may deem most proper. In large or important bodies he is usually styled *Secretary*.

It is the duty of the recording officer to make a true entry of the proceedings of the assembly. But this does not include the speeches of members. But it includes everything voted or ordered by the assembly, either by express vote or general consent, which is in general to the same effect as an express vote.

It is in general the duty of the Secretary or recording officer to read all papers coming before the assembly for its information. When a member in debate or other occasion desires the reading of a paper for information of the assembly, he should send it to the Secretary for that purpose. It can be read by a member only on leave or general consent of the assembly, which in practice is considered as granted, when no objection is made.

It is the duty of the Secretary to call the roll of the assembly, whenever a call is ordered, and take a note of those who are absent, and to call the names of members when a question is taken by yeas and nays and note the answers of members. To notify committees of their appointment and inform them as to the matters referred to them, and to authenticate in connection with the President all acts and proceedings of the assembly.

The Secretary is charged with the custody of all papers and documents of the assembly, and the journals or minutes of its proceedings.

It being the duty of the presiding officer to announce the result of every vote or action of the assembly, the Secretary is expected to be guided thereby in recording its proceedings.

To this extent the Secretary is under the control and direction of the presiding officer in discharging this branch of his duties subject to revision or correction by vote of the assembly.

The Secretary should stand while reading papers or calling the assembly or while engaged in like duties.

## PUBLIC MEETINGS.

In many of the States of the Union, counties are divided into districts, styled towns or townships, the inhabitants thereof becoming bodies corporate. In towns under the system called township organizations, as existing in the New England States, and some of the Northern and Western States, the law provides for stated meetings of the electors, called town meetings, for the consideration of town affairs. In the absence of any provision to the contrary these assemblies conduct their proceedings according to the rules of parliamentary law.

In many of the States, as in New York, Michigan, Illinois and Wisconsin, there exists a county board for the management and control of county affairs, called *Board of Supervisors,* which is composed of representatives or delegates from each of the several towns of the county. These boards thus formed are deliberative assemblies, and as such their proceedings are subject to the rules of parliamentary law the same as other like assemblies. And the same is true of City and Town Councils in the various cities and towns of the country.

Societies and secret orders, as Free Masons, Odd Fellows, charitable and literary societies, and the like, being in their nature deliberative assemblies, their proceedings are in general conducted under the rules of parliamentary law.

Public meetings by voluntary assent are of daily occurrence. These meetings are sometimes convened at the instance of committees appointed for that purpose; and are frequently convened at the request of citizens who desire such meeting, on public notice, either by hand-bill notices posted, or by notice in a newspaper.

## ORGANIZATION OF PUBLIC MEETINGS.

The first business at a public meeting is its organization. This is effected by choosing a presiding officer to keep order, and a Secretary to record the proceedings of the meeting, after which it is competent for the meeting to choose such other officers as may be deemed necessary. In case the meeting is composed of a very large number of persons, the presiding officer is called *President;* if not he is usually styled *Chairman* of the meeting.

When the people have assembled, and the hour of meeting arrives, the meeting should be called to order. In case the meeting has been convened at the instance of a committee, the Chairman or person first named on the committee should call the meeting to order. In case it was convened at the instance of citizens, the first named on the list should assume this duty, otherwise, the proper person for this purpose would be the Mayor of the city, or principal public officer, or most prominent person present.

The person calling the meeting to order should take such position in the room as to command the attention of the audience, and announce as follows: "Gentlemen, the hour at which this meeting is to convene having arrived, it is proposed that we proceed to organize; I therefore nominate Mr. A. B. as chairman." The nomination being seconded, he proceeds: "Gentlemen, those who are in favor of such nomination, will say 'aye'; those opposed will say 'no.'" The vote being taken, if carried in the affirmative, he will say, "It is carried in the affirmative," or "it is agreed to; Mr. A. B. is chosen chairman of this meeting; will he please come forward and take the chair?"

If the meeting is deemed one of importance so that the position of Chairman would be deemed one of considerable honor, it is customary for the presiding officer to return thanks to the meeting for the honor conferred; this he will do on taking the chair.*

---

\* An example of brevity in a speech of this kind is found in the following address of Newton Cloud on

## Organization of Public Meetings. 37

As every deliberative body should have a Secretary before the meeting can be considered fully organized, the Chairman will say, "Gentlemen, the first business in order will be the election of a Secretary." If no other person moves, the person who called the meeting to order should also nominate a Secretary; but any person present may make such nomination.

The Secretary being chosen, the further business will be directed by the meeting. If the meeting is called for some particular purpose, it is proper in selecting a

---

being chosen President of the Constitutional Convention of Illinois in 1847:

*Gentlemen of the Convention:* It is but proper on entering upon the duty assigned by the choice just made, that I should return you my most sincere thanks for the honor you have conferred. I enter upon the discharge of the duties of President of this convention with much embarrassment, for I feel that I have a difficult and important duty assigned me. I can only promise that my best efforts shall be made to discharge that duty faithfully and impartially, and that all the little ability I possess shall be devoted to the despatch and furtherence of the public business. I will not allude, however remotely, to the great subjects upon which we have been called to act, but will conclude by returning you again my sincere thanks for the honor you have conferred on me.

Chairman to choose some person best acquainted with the object of the meeting; if this is the case, the Chairman should proceed after the election of Secretary and state the object of the meeting. If not, he should say, "The chair is not fully advised as to the object of this meeting. It will be proper that the object of the meeting be stated by some person to whom it is best known." It will be generally understood who this person is, and a motion may be made calling on him for that purpose, or he may be called out by several voices.

It will be proper for the meeting to choose one or more Vice-Presidents, and one or more Assistant Secretaries. This is done where the meeting is large—generally as a means of manifesting the importance of the occasion. They will also choose such committees as may be deemed necessary.

When an assembly is composed of delegates chosen by and representing others, the organization is, in the first instance, considered temporary, upon which measures are taken to ascertain who are members; this is usually done by the appointment of a committee to examine the credentials of those claiming to be members, and to report accordingly.

Until this is done there is a presumption that all present who assume to take part in the assembly are entitled to do so, as it is supposed that no gentleman would be guilty of imposition in this respect. At the time of appointing the committee on credentials, it is customary also to appoint a committee to report the names of persons for permanent officers of the assembly or convention.

After the report of the committee on credentials is adopted, the assembly, on motion of some member, proceeds to the election of permanent officers. If the names of candidates have been recommended by a committee, the adoption of their report is regarded as making choice of the persons they have recommended. In the case of an assembly composed of delegates, unless it is an important occasion, it is not customary for the Temporary Chairman to return thanks to the convention, or to allude to the object of the meeting; he simply acts as Moderator for the time being, for purpose of organization.

In case the assembly or convention is small, it is customary, after the temporary organization is perfected and the question of membership is settled, to declare by vote that the temporary organization shall stand as the permanent organization.*

When the organization of the meeting is completed by the election of officers, the Chairman should announce, "The meeting is now fully organized, and ready to proceed to business." If no motion is made or business presented, it is proper for the Chairman to say, "What is the pleasure of the meeting?" And at any time when there is no business before the meeting, the Chairman should announce, "Gentlemen, there is no question before the meeting; what is your further pleasure?"

---

* When the assembly is composed of delegates from constituencies, a temporary organization becomes necessary to determine who are properly delegates and entitled to seats in the convention. But in mass meetings of the people, such necessity does not in general exist, hence a reason why the original organization in the latter case may be accepted as permanent.

## Manner of Presenting Business.

Every member of a deliberative body, in the absence of express rule to the contrary, has the right to present propositions for the action of the assembly. This is by a simple *motion* or by formal resolution. But where the object of the meeting is of a general nature, or where the subject designed to be acted upon, for which the meeting has been called, does not seem to have been duly matured by any one present, it is customary to appoint a committee to prepare and report resolutions expressive of the sense of the meeting.

When a member desires to present a proposition for the action of the assembly which is of importance, it should properly be reduced to writing; such propositions are called resolutions, and commence thus: "*Resolved*, That." Indeed as a general rule all propositions offered by members in a deliberative assembly, except a mere motion in the progress of proceedings, should be reduced to writing.

## Motions, and Manner of Proceeding.

A motion is simply a proposition of a member, as his individual sentiments. If the proposition offered prevails, it is then adopted as the conclusion or sense of the assembly.

But the proposition by a single member is not considered sufficient to claim attention from the assembly; it is, therefore, required that it shall be approved or *seconded* by one other member. This being done, the mover is entitled to have it put to the assembly. In general practice, however, all motions are presumed to be seconded, unless the point is made and found to be otherwise; in which case the presiding officer could not properly take notice of the motion.

In good practice, when a motion is made, the presiding officer is not required, indeed, it is not necessary that he should stop to enquire as to whether the motion has a second, in case he fails to hear any person announce that he seconds the motion. He may assume that the motion has a second until the contrary is made to appear. This is the custom in legislative assemblies or large bodies where it is necessary to economize time. The seconding of a motion has become largely a matter of form, although it is the right of any member to raise the point of order in case a motion has not the support of a second.

In general, no proposition or question can be acted upon except on *motion* of a member. The manner of proceeding is for the member to rise in his place, and say, "Mr. Chairman." Before he can proceed it is expected that he will have the permission, or as it is termed, "recognition of the chair." The Chairman, therefore, responds: "The gentleman from," naming the district from which he is a delegate, or, "the gentleman on my right," or similar designations. The rule in deliberative assemblies being that no member shall be addressed or spoken of by his *name* where it can be avoided. The person offering the motion, being recognized by the Chair, proceeds, "I move, sir, that," stating his motion. The member desiring to *second* the motion should rise and say, "I second the motion." Before any remarks upon the motion or proposition are in order, it must be stated by the chair. The Chairman should say, "Gentlemen, it is moved that" (stating the substance of the motion). It is sometimes the practice for the Chairman to say, "Gentlemen, you have heard the motion," and then proceed to put the question. But this is improper; a motion is not the property of the assembly, or, in other words, not a subject before them, until it is *stated* by the Chairman.

When a motion is made and seconded, it becomes the property of the assembly, and cannot be withdrawn or modified by the mover except by leave of the assembly, on a motion made for that purpose.

After the Chairman has stated a motion, which he may do without rising, if no member interposes, he should proceed promptly to put the question to the assembly; this he does by rising, when he will say, "Gentlemen, those in favor of the motion will say *aye*"—" those opposed will say *no*."

If it is decided in the affirmative, he will say, "The motion has prevailed," or, "It is carried in the affirmative." If it is decided in the negative, he will say, "The motion is lost," or, "It is decided in the negative."

After the vote has been declared by the presiding officer, it becomes final. Sometimes, when the vote is nearly equal, it is difficult to determine which has prevailed. In such case the presiding officer should not hastily announce the vote. He should say, "The ayes *seem* to have it," or, "The noes *seem* to have it," as the vote may appear. If no member interposes, he may then proceed and declare the vote as it seems to him to be.

But if any member doubts the vote as the Chairman states that it seems to be, he may rise and call for a division of the house. This may be done, as the call indicates, by dividing the members of the assembly—by having those who vote in the affirmative stand on one side of the room, and those in the negative stand on the opposite side; or by the "up-lifted hand"—the latter is the most usual—or simply by rising. In either case the Chairman will direct the Secretary to count the votes on each side, and report to him the result. The most usual and satisfactory course is by rising.

When a member calls for a division of the house, in the absence of any express rule made by the assembly on the subject, the presiding officer should proceed thus: "A division is called for; all those in favor of the motion will rise in their place, and stand until counted." When those in the affirmative are counted, and the number is reported to the Chairman, he will announce the number, and say: "All those opposed to the motion will in like manner rise and stand until counted," which being done, the Chairman announces the number, and declares the motion carried or lost according to the fact. The Chairman may himself count the vote, if he desires, but it is competent for him to direct the Secretary to do so.

In case any member desires it, he may, at any time before the vote is declared by the Chairman, call for the appointment of *tellers* to count and report the result of the vote, instead of leaving it to the Chairman. This is done by the Chairman on request of any member. It is customary to appoint one person from each side, or each party in the assembly. When a division is desired, it must be called for before the result has been finally declared by the Chairman. After he has declared the vote, it is final, and a division cannot be called for.

## Motions in General.

When a motion is made which the members are inclined to meet by a direct vote, on the merits, it is put to the assembly, either at once or after debate, and disposed of. But as propositions may strike different minds in different forms, it often occurs that the assembly, on motion of some member, will dispose of the question in some other manner; for this purpose there is a class of motions resorted to, called *subsidiary* motions, which may be entertained while the original or principal motion is pending, thus:

1. The assembly may desire to suppress the proposition, either for a time or altogether. The proper subsidiary motions for this purpose are, the *previous question* and *indefinite postponement*.

2. The assembly may be wi'ling to consider the proposition, *but not at that time*. The usual motions in such case are, *postponement* to some future time, or to *lie on the table*.

3. The form in which the proposition is submitted may be considered defective in some particular, a correction of which may require more deliberate consideration than the assembly can conveniently bestow upon it. In such case the proper motion is to *refer* the proposition *to a committee*.

4. The proposition of itself may be satisfactory, if changed or qualified in some particular. In this case the proper motion is *to amend*.

## The Previous Question.

The practice under this motion has not been uniform. In legislative assemblies it is generally regulated by rules prescribed; the usual course, however, in the absence of express rules, is this: When a member desires a vote to be taken on a proposition without further debate or delay, he moves the *previous question*, this being seconded, the presiding officer says, "The previous question is moved. Shall the main question be now put? Those in favor will say 'aye,'—those opposed will say 'no.'" If carried in the affirmative, he will say, "The main question is ordered." In this case the assembly must come to a direct vote on the main question, without debate, and no motion can be entertained to dispose of the question in any other manner; the *main question* is the original proposition, with pending amendments if any, each of which is to be disposed of in its proper order. If the motion for the previous question is lost, or decided in the negative, the general rule is stated to be, that the main question is taken out of the assembly for the day, so that there is then nothing before it to postpone, commit or amend.*

---

\* Cushing's Manual, § 175. But in Illinois the practice is that the main question is still pending as if no vote had been taken.

### Indefinite Postponement.

This motion is decided without debate. If in the affirmative it removes the question from before the assembly as effectually as if it had never been pending. A motion to postpone to a day beyond the sitting of the assembly is of the same effect as indefinite postponement.

### Motion to Postpone or Lie on the Table.

When it is desired to consider a proposition at some future day, the proper motion is to *postpone* or *lay on the table*. The motion to postpone in this case has reference to a motion to postpone to a time fixed; in this respect it differs from the motion to lay on the table. When a proposition is postponed to a time fixed, when that time arrives it will be in order to resume its consideration, but a proposition which by vote is laid on the table, its consideration cannot be resumed without a vote to that effect.

A proposition which has been laid upon the table may be taken up at any time for consideration by vote of the assembly, unless there is some special rule prescribed by the assembly to the contrary. The opinion has been entertained to some extent that when a proposition is laid upon the table it is a final disposition of the question, and its consideration can not be again resumed. But this is so only where there is some special rule of the assembly to that effect. The rule of the English Parliament as cited by Mr. Jefferson is that "where the House has something else which claims its present attention, but would be willing to reserve in their power to take up a proposition whenever it shall suit them, they order it to lie on their table. It may then be called for at any time."

But a motion to take from the table a proposition which has been laid on the table by vote of the assembly would not come under the head of privileged motions, so this motion could not properly be entertained while some particular order of business or some other principal motion is pending.

The technical motion to lie on the table is

not recognized in the legislative assemblies in some of the States of the Union; but the equivalent motion "to postpone for the present" is used in its stead.

## MOTION TO COMMIT.

When it is desired to render a proposition more perfect before consideration, it is usually done by referring it to a committee. If there is a *standing* committee on that subject, the motion should be to refer to that committee. If not, then to a *select* committee. A motion to refer to a select committee, and a standing committee, may be made and pending at the same time; in which case, the latter motion takes precedence, and should be first put to the question. A part or the whole of a subject may be referred; or portions may be referred to several different committees.

After a motion to commit a proposition under consideration, a motion to amend the proposition is not in order, but in the absence of any special rule of the assembly to the contrary the motion itself may be amended by substituting another committee for that named in the motion, or by enlarging or diminishing the number of the committee when the motion is to refer to a select committee—naming the number of the committee. And the committee may on motion be instructed among other things as to their action on the proposition committed to them, which may in effect operate as an amendment thereto.

If the motion to commit is carried in the affirmative, the effect is to remove the whole subject to which the motion relates from before the assembly for the time being.

## Motions to Amend.

Amending a proposition is either by adding words, or taking words from it, or by transposition of words. This is accomplished under different modes of proceeding. Under this head may be classed the following:

### 1. Filling Blanks.

It often happens that propositions are

introduced, leaving blanks to be filled by the assembly, either with times and numbers, or with provisions analogous to those of the proposition itself. In the latter case, blanks are filled in the same way that other amendments are made by the insertion of words. In the former, propositions to fill blanks are not considered as amendments to the question, but as original motions, to be made and decided before the principal question.

In case of blanks to be filled with *time* and *number*, motions may be made for that purpose, and the question taken on each by itself. Several motions for this purpose may be made and pending, before any of them are put to the question. The usual rule is to take the question, first, on the *highest number*, the *largest sum*, and the *longest time*.

Whilst the foregoing is the general rule on this subject, it is nevertheless to be applied in the light of a further general rule; to commence at that point on which the assembly would be the least likely to concur, and go towards that on which the minds of members would in the nature of things be most likely to unite, or as it has been expressed, "The object being not to begin at that extreme which and more being within every man's wish, no one could negative it, and yet, if we should vote in the affirmative, every question for more would be precluded; but at that extreme which would unite few, and then to advance or recede till you get to a number which will unite a bare majority.*

## 2. Striking Out.

If an amendment is proposed by striking out a paragraph or certain words, and it is rejected, it cannot be again moved to strike out the same words, nor a part of them; but it may be moved to strike out the same words with others, or to strike out a part of the same words with others, provided it becomes thereby a different proposition.

## 3. Amendment by Inserting.

If an amendment is proposed by insert-

---

* 3 Grey, 376.

ing or adding a paragraph or words, and it is rejected, it cannot be again moved to insert the same words, or a part of them; but it may be moved to insert the same with others, or a part of the same words with others, if the coherence really make them different propositions.

### 4. Striking Out and Inserting.

This combination of propositions may be divided by a vote of the assembly. When the proposition is divided, the question is first to be taken on striking out; if that prevails, then on inserting; if the former is decided in the negative, the latter fails of course.

### 5. Division of a Proposition

Where a proposition is composed of two or more parts, which are susceptible of division into several questions, it is a compendious mode of amendment to divide the motion, if deemed devisable, into separate questions, to be separately voted upon. This may be done by order of the assembly, on motion, as in other cases. The question as divided becomes a series of independent propositions. Assemblies sometimes provide by express rule for the division of a question on demand of a member.

The rule before mentioned for division of a question on demand of a member has led to a misunderstanding to some extent as to the course to be pursued in regard to such proceeding. The understanding by some has been that the term "demand of a member" means that on demand of a member therefor, it becomes the duty of the presiding officer to proceed himself and divide the question in manner and according to the demand of the members. The rules of parliamentary law give no such right to a member of a deliberative assembly, nor do they confer any such authority as suggested upon the presiding officer.

Whilst the division of a question is in the nature of an amendment, yet to a certain extent the proceeding is taken out of the general rules governing in this regard. So that a question may be pending where an amendment, or further amendment offered by a member, would not be in order, but the question being in such form as to admit of a division, the object of the rule is to permit a division that complete justice may be done towards all who may be called upon to vote on the proposition. So while a member who desires a division would not be permitted under the general rules in regard to amendments to offer amendments so as to modify the proposition and thereby put it in shape as he desires, he may nevertheless demand a division of the question. That is, move that the question be divided, which is made a sort of privileged motion.

On demand or motion of a member for division of a proposition, the presiding officer puts the question to the assembly for its decision as in other cases. The presiding officer may decide whether the proposition is susceptible of division and how many and what parts it may be divided into, but from this decision there would be an appeal as in other cases of his ruling, unless there is a special rule of the assembly giving such authority to the presiding officer. Mr. Jefferson, citing English authority, says: "If a question contain more parts than one, it may be divided into two or more questions. But not as the right of an individual member, but with the consent of the House."

6. AMENDMENT TO AN AMENDMENT.

Custom or usage has established a rule whereby a proposition may be entertained to amend an amendment, but there can be no amendment of an amendment to an amendment.

## THE ORDER AND SUCCESSION OF QUESTIONS.

It is a general rule that where a proposition is pending before a deliberative assembly no other can be entertained until that is disposed of, unless it be either: *first*, a privileged question; *secondly*, an incidental question; or, *thirdly*, a subsidiary question or motion.*

---

* The House of Representatives in the Illinois Legislature, has the following rule: "When a question is under debate, no motion shall be received but to adjourn, a call

## 1. Privileged Questions.

Questions of this nature are: 1. Motions to adjourn. 2. Motions or questions relating to the rights and privileges of the assembly, or of its members individually. 3. Motions for the orders of the day.

*A motion to adjourn* takes the place of all other questions whatever. It is not debateable, and ordinarily not susceptible of amendent.

A motion to adjourn to a time fixed can be amended, by offering some other time, and is debateable.

*Questions of privilege* come next in order, and take precedence of all other motions except that of adjournment. They are such as concern the rights and privileges of the assembly, or of its individual members.

---

of the house, to lay on the table, the previous question, to commit, to amend, to postpone to a day certain, to postpone indefinitely; which several motions shall have precedence in the order in which they are arranged; and no motion to postpone to a day certain, to commit, or postpone indefinitely, being decided, shall be again allowed on the same day, and at the same stage of the bill or proposition."

*Orders of the day* come thirdly in succession, under the head of privileged questions. When the consideration of a subject has been assigned for a particular day, by an order of the assembly, the matter so assigned is called the order of the day for that day.

## 2. Incidental Questions.

These are such as arise out of other questions, consequently are to be decided before those which give rise to them. Of this nature are: 1. Questions of order; 2. Motions for the reading of papers, etc.; 3. Leave to withdraw a motion; 4. Suspension of a rule; 5. Amendment of an amendment.

*Questions of order* are those questions raised by any member as to a breach of any rule, occurring. It is the privilege of any member to raise questions of order in such cases.

*Reading of papers* brought before a deliberative assembly may be called for by any member who desires the reading.

*Withdrawal of motions* is allowed on the

part of the mover, by leave of the assembly, which is to be obtained by a vote on motion as in other cases, or the leave may be obtained by general consent without a formal vote of the assembly.

*Suspension of a rule* of the assembly may be granted by a vote thereof. This is usually obtained at the instance of a member to consider a proposition which would otherwise not be in order.

*Amendment of an amendment* is allowable, as we have already seen; the amendment to the amendment must be first put. If it is adopted, then the question is taken on the amendment as amended.

### 3. Subsidiary Questions.

These, as before remarked, are those which relate to a principal motion. Subsidiary motions in common use are: to lie on the table; the previous question; postponement, either indefinitely or to a day certain; commitment and amendment.

*To lie on the table,* is a motion usually resorted to in common practice when the assembly desire to put a proposition aside without giving any expression upon its merits. It is not debatable nor susceptible of amendment. It takes precedence of and supersedes all other subsidiary motions. If decided in the affirmative, all motions or propositions connected with the principal question, are removed with it from before the assembly, until taken up by a vote thereof.

*The previous question* stands in equal degree with all other subsidiary motions, except the motion to lie on the table.

*The motion to postpone* is either indefinite, or to a time certain; and in both these forms, may be amended;—in the former by fixing a time certain; in the latter by substituting one time for another. The latter case is treated like filling blanks.

*A motion to commit,* or recommit, may be amended by substitution of one kind of committee for another, or by enlarging or diminishing the number of the committee as proposed, or by instructions to the committee.* It stands in the same degree with

---

* See remarks on the motion to commit, ante p. 53.

the previous question and postponement—but it takes precedence of a motion to amend.

*A motion to amend* stands in the same degree only with the previous question and indefinite postponement, and neither, if first moved, is superseded by the other. But it is liable to be superseded by a motion to postpone to a day certain. It may also be superseded by a motion to commit.

*The following example* is given to illustrate the successive order of questions: Suppose *first* a principal question is proposed, *second*, a motion is made to amend the principal question, *third*, a motion to commit, *fourth*, a question of order arises in the debate, which gives occasion to, *fifth*, a question of privilege, and *sixth*, a subsidiary motion, as to lie on the table. All these questions may be pending at the same time, and take rank in the order named. The regular course of proceeding requires the motion to lie on the table to be first put. If this is negatived, the question of privilege is then settled; after that comes the question of order, then the question of commitment; if that is negatived, the question of amendment is taken; and, lastly, the main question.

## OF RECONSIDERATION.

A deliberative assembly may reconsider a vote already passed, whether affirmatively or negatively. For this purpose a motion is made, as in other cases, that such a vote be reconsidered; if it prevails, the matter stands before the assembly in precisely the same state and condition as if the vote reconsidered had never been passed. In the absence of any express rule of the assembly, a motion to reconsider is made in the same manner as any other motion.

Reconsideration of questions once disposed of by vote of the assembly is of American origin. The general rule existing, time out of mind, in the English Parliament is that a question once carried cannot be questioned again at the same session, but must stand as the judgment of the house. And a bill once rejected, another of the same substance cannot be brought in again the same session.

The reconsideration of questions seems to have been adopted in deliberative assemblies in this country somewhat on the principle that new trials are granted to litigants in courts of law. But a motion to reconsider being decided in the negative is a final disposition of the question.

A motion to reconsider a proposition is entertained without regard to whether it was determined in the affirmative or negative. As before remarked, the motion is made in the usual manner of any other motion. In the absence of any special rule of the assembly to the contrary, it may be made by any member of the assembly.*

---

\* The opinion seems to prevail quite generally that a motion to reconsider a proposition must be made by some member of the assembly who voted with the majority on the question. There is no such rule of parliementary law. There is, however, a special rule to this effect in Congress, and the like rule has been adopted among the legislative assemblies of the several States.

There is likewise a practice prevailing in deliberative assemblies, that where a motion to reconsider is made to move to lay the motion to reconsider on the table, which being carried in the affirmative, the notion is entertained that by some rule of parliamentary law the main ques-

It is said by writers of parliamentary law who are recognized as authority in this country, that on the motion to reconsider, the whole subject is as much open for debate as if it had not been discussed at all.*

But it would seem that on such motions the debate ought to be confined more particularly to direct reasons showing why the vote should or should not be reconsidered. Something of this kind might naturally exist in the case aside from the naked question of the original merits of the proposition. If the motion to reconsider prevails, the question pending will then be on the original proposition the same as it stood before any vote thereon was taken, and in like manner again open to debate. The question should be stated by the chair and put to vote in the same manner as before.

---

tion is finally disposed of so that it cannot be again entertained by the assembly. This is incorrect. There is no general rule existing that would prevent the subject from being taken from the table again as in case of any other question. But legislative assemblies generally have some special rule on the subject which virtually makes such action final.

\* Cushing's Manual, ¿ 337.

## Of Committees.

The business of deliberative assemblies is facilitated by aid of committees; they are of three kinds, *select committees, standing committees,* and *committee of the whole.*

*Select committees* are those appointed to consider a particular subject.

*Standing committees* are those who are appointed to continue during the whole term of the assembly, to consider all matters of a certain character named during the time.

*A committee of the whole* is a committee comprising all the members of the assembly to consider any subject referred to them.

Select and standing committees, in the absence of any express rule or vote of the assembly, are appointed by the presiding officer. When a motion is made for the appointment of a committee, the motion usually includes the number of which it is to consist. If no vote is taken as to the manner of appointment, the presiding officer should proceed to appoint. It will be unnecessary for him to inquire of the assembly as to how they will have the appointment made; the fact that they have given no expression on the subject implies that the appointment shall be made by the chair.

The person first named on a committee is considered the chairman; but in the absence of any rule to the contrary, the committee may make choice of some other person among their number as chairman, if they desire to do so.

When a committee have considered a proposition, they present the result to the assembly, which is called their *report.* It is usually in writing, and is announced to the assembly by the chairman, or some member of the committee selected for that purpose, who, rising in his place, says, "Mr. President" (or "Mr. Chairman," as the case may be), "The committee to whom was "referred the subject of (stating the matter "referred), have had the same under con-"sideration, and have instructed me to "report that" (here follows the report.)

In case the report is in writing the foregoing is the proper form for the caption or commencement. The report need not be addressed to any one. The practice of addressing a report to the presiding officer or to the assembly in the manner of a bill in chancery or petition from outside sources is erroneous. When the report goes into the journal of the proceedings of the assembly it will be found to connect with that which precedes or follows it sufficiently and even in better taste without the addition of a needless and cumbersome address. The report is a part of the proceedings of the assembly.

Where communications come from outside parties the rule is different. Such matters have no legitimate connection with the record of the assembly and some address or introduction of that nature seems to be necessary. But a committee is a part of the assembly and the rule applicable to strangers in this regard has no application to them. The report of a committee being in the nature of a continuation of the proceedings of the assembly, the inconsistency of adding thereto a formal address is at once apparent.

It is the duty of a committee when a matter is referred to them, to act upon it The object of a reference of this kind is to procure an examination into the merits of the proposition so referred. It is the duty of the committee to report the result of their examination of the question and add their recommendations, which should be either for or against the same. They will fail to discharge their duty properly should they not do this.

The committee may, however, in case they wish to escape responsibility of this kind report the matter back without recommendation and ask to be discharged from consideration of the subject. But the assembly may refuse this request, in which case it will be the duty of the committee to add to their report their opinion of the measure. The assembly may, however, discharge them and refer the matter to another committee.

It is highly improper in a committee instead of a recommendation upon the merits of the subject, to recommend that the matter be referred to some other committee, or that it lie upon the table, or other dillitory course. Such recommendation is not within the province of a committee. They must in their report either deal with the merits of the question or ask to be discharged from its further consideration. If their application to be discharged is concurred in by the assembly, then it would be proper for the chairman of the committee from his place as a member to move that the subject be referred to some other committee, or other disposition thereof as may be desired.

After the report is made, the proper motion is, that it be received; but in practice the report is received without such motion, unless objection is made, in which case a formal vote on the reception of the report is necessary. After the report is received, the committee are discharged without any action of the assembly.

The report thereupon becomes the property of the assembly, and the question recurs on its adoption. The presiding officer will proceed and so state the question, without any formal motion being made. The report being accepted, the question recurs on its adoption. After a report is adopted, the recommendation of the committee becomes the sense of the assembly.

## Committee of the Whole.

A committee of the whole is a meeting or session of all the members of the assembly, in which the strict rules of order governing the assembly itself in the despatch of business are dispensed with, thereby affording more freedom of action in deliberating on subjects under consideration. In the House of Representatives in Congress and in legislative assemblies in general it is styled *committee of the whole house.*

In many legislative assemblies this committee exists by a standing rule, and all bills before being advanced to final consideration are referred to and are required to be considered by the committee of the whole. The mode of proceeding being to consider each bill or proposition by sections or paragraphs.

In the absence of any special rule to the contrary it is proper for the assembly to resolve itself into committee of the whole on any proposition pending, or on several propositions as may be deemed advisable.

The mode of proceeding on going into committee of the whole is on motion of some member that "the assembly do now resolve itself into the committee of the whole for the purpose of considering the subject of" (naming the subject.) Before this motion is made, however, it is proper that the assembly, on motion, should vote to refer the subject named to such committee.

If the motion to go into committee of the whole prevails, it is customary for the presiding officer of the assembly to designate some member to act as Chairman of the committee. But the committee may, it seems, disregard the designation by the presiding officer and select a Chairman for itself. This proceeding, however, is in general regulated by special rule of the assembly.

According to the rule laid down by Mr.

Cushing, in case no person is named by the presiding officer as Chairman, or the committee do not acquiese in his appointment, some member is called upon by one or more members of the committee to take the Chair; and if no objection is made, the member so designated becomes the Chairman. If objection is made or some other member is also named as Chairman, then a Chairman must be regularly chosen But in order to do this the presiding officer should resume the Chair, and the choice be made by the assembly acting as such, and not in committee.*

In organizing the committee of the whole, nothing further is necessary than the selection of a Chairman. But for convenience and to relieve the burdens of the Chairman in this regard, some one of the committee may be designated to act as Clerk, or the Clerk of the assembly may be requested to act in that capacity. It is

---

\* See Cushing's Manual, ¿ 340. So that the authority of the committee of the whole to select its own Chairman depends, it seems, upon the contingency of unanimity of its action in the matter.

not, however, his duty to do so by virtue of his position.

The meeting of the committee of the whole is in the same room occupied by the assembly. On going into committee the presiding officer of the assembly takes his seat among the members. If he is himself a member of the assembly, he takes part in the debates and deliberations of the committee the same as other members. A quorum is the same as in the assembly. If at any time it is found that there is not a quorum present, the committee should rise and report the fact to the assembly for its action.

The Chairman of the committee in assuming his duties as such usually takes a seat at the desk of the Clerk or Secretary of the assembly, when he will announce, "The assembly is now in committee of the whole on the subject of," (naming the subject). If the proposition consists of several sections or paragraphs, the same should be considered separately, beginning with the first in number, which should be read by the Chairman in their proper order.

After reading each it is open to amendment.

After amendment of a section or paragraph, or in case no amendments are offered, the question recurs on its adoption. It being adopted or rejected, the Chairman passes on through the whole subject in like manner, which being completed the question recurs on adoption of the entire proposition as a whole.

Whilst a committee of the whole is in form and its proceedings are in general after the manner of deliberative assemblies, yet but few of the rules of parliamentary law governing deliberative assemblies are applicable to proceedings in committee of the whole. *Privileged, subsidiary* and *incidental* questions are in general not recognized, especially those of a dilatory character. The policy being to proceed to a direct vote on the main question.

Mr. Cushing in his manual of Parliamentary practice, has laid down the following general rules concerning committee of the whole. 1. The previous question cannot be moved in committees of the whole. 2. The committee cannot like other committees adjourn to some other time and place. 3. Every member can speak in the committee as often as he can obtain the floor. 4. A committee of the whole cannot refer a matter to another committee. 5. A committee of the whole has no authority to punish for a breach of order committed by any one.*

To the foregoing rules it may be added that neither can the yeas and nays be demanded in committee of the whole. And it is laid down that no appeal can be entertained from the decision of the Chair, his decision being final on points of order.†

It was formerly the practice when it was desired to terminate prolonged or unprofitable debate on a question in committee of the whole for the committee to rise and report the facts to the assembly, when the assembly could withdraw the subject from

---

\* Cushing's Manual, § 302. A committee of the whole having no authority to enforce rules, would imply that they are wanting in authority to make rules for their government.

† Matthias Manual, 66.

the committee and dispose of the same itself if deemed advisable. But latterly the practice instead of the former course has obtained to entertain a motion to close debate on the pending question, which answers the same effect as the previous question.

If the committee desire to adjourn their sitting to another time before disposing of the matter referred to them, instead of the proceeding by adjournment, the rule is for the committee to rise, whereupon the presiding officer of the assembly resumes his place and the chairman of the committee reports, "The committee of the whole to which was referred the (stating the subject) have had the same under consideration, and have instructed me to report that they have made some progress therein, and respectfully ask leave to sit again."*

The presiding officer should state the substance of the report to the assembly, and may thereupon add, "If there is no

---

* On a second report of this kind the report should be "some *further* progress," etc.

objection leave will be granted." If no one objects, he will add "Leave is granted." If objections are heard the question recurs on concurring in the request of the committee, which should he put to a vote of the assembly as in case of any other motion.

In case of disturbance or disorderly conduct on the part of members or among spectators, instead of punishment for contempt the rule is for the committee to rise and report the facts to the assembly for its action.

No record of the proceedings of a committee of the whole is required to be kept. It is sufficient to preserve a memorandum of propositions adopted or rejected or amendments adopted, if any, whereby the action of the committee may be made known to the assembly. Nor need the proceedings of the committee appear in the journal of the proceedings of the assembly. All that is required in this regard is that it shall appear that the assembly resolved itself into committee of the whole, stating the subject referred, followed by the report of the committee and action of the assembly thereon.

When the committee of the whole have finally disposed of the matter referred to them, they should recommend, as in case of other committees, that the proposition either be adopted or rejected. If amendments have been proposed by the committee, the recommendation will be that the proposition as amended be adopted.

In the latter case the report of the Chairman will be, "The committee of the whole to which was referred the (naming the subject) have had the same under consideration and have instructed me to report said proposition back with sundry amendments proposed thereto, and that they recommend the adoption of the same as amended." In case no amendment is proposed, then say, "Report said proposition back without amendment and that they recommend the adoption of the same," or "recommend that the same be not adopted." In case of a bill in a legislative assembly, the conclusion of such report will be "that said bill do pass," or "that said bill do not pass."

C

## Appeals.

As a general rule as before expressed in this work, the presiding officer of a deliberative assembly possesses little or no power whatever;* the theory being that all power and authority is vested in the assembly itself, which is transferred to the presiding officer only by special rule. In general all decisions and rulings of the presiding officer may be reviewed and reversed by the assembly itself through an appeal on a question of order raised by any member.†

A question of order raised by a member is not like other questions stated by the Chair, but must be stated to the Chair by the member by whom it is raised. It is decided in the first instance by the presiding officer without debate or discussion. The presiding officer may, however, before giving his decision invite the opinion and advice of such experienced members present as he deems proper.

---

\* See ante page 28.

† It is the rule in the English Parliament that all decisions of the Speaker may be controlled by the House. 3 Grey, 319.

If the decision of the presiding officer on the question raised is not satisfactory, any member may except to it and demand that it be decided by the assembly. This is called an *appeal* from the decision of the Chair. The mode of proceeding thereupon is for the presiding officer to proceed and state the question of order raised, and conclude, " shall the decision of the Chair stand as the decision of the assembly." The question is thereupon open to debate and decision of the assembly the same as any other question. The presiding officer is allowed to participate in the debate.*

## Of Debate.

Among other branches of parliamentary law, certain rules of order in debate be-

---

\* Experienced parliamentarians understand that large advantage is gained in obtaining the affirmative of a question. Mankind not being in general aggressive in their nature it is easier to say *yes* than it is to say *no*. Thus the chances are in favor of an affirmative vote; so in cases of appeals, good practice inclines members who favor the decision of the Chair to move that the appeal be laid upon the table, which is a proper motion in parliamentary practice.

came established in the English Parliament, which are recognized as applicable in deliberative bodies in this country. These rules as laid down by Mr. Jefferson citing authorities, are to the following effect.

When the Speaker is seated in his chair, every member is to sit in his place. When any member desires to speak, he is to stand up in his place, and address himself, not to the House or any particular member, but to the Speaker, who calls him by his name that the House may take notice who it is that speaks. But members who are indisposed may speak sitting.*

When a member stands up to speak, no question is to be put; but he is to be heard unless the House overrule.† If two or more rise to speak nearly together, the Speaker determines who was first up, and calls him by name; whereupon he proceeds,

---

\* In legislative assemblies in this country the Speaker in recognizing a member who rises to address the Chair, does so by announcing the locality he represents, as ' the gentleman from ———.''

† The rule recognized in this country, is that when a member rises to speak and has obtained the floor by recognition of the presiding officer, he is entitled to proceed unless he forfeits his right by some breach of order.

unless he voluntarily sits down and gives way to another. But sometimes the House does not acquiesce in the Speaker's decision, in which case the question is put "which member was first up."*

No member can speak more than once to the same bill on the same day; or even on another day, if the debate be adjourned. But if it be read more than once on the same day, he may speak once at every reading. Even a change of opinion does not give a right to be heard a second time.

But a member may be permitted to speak again to clear a matter of fact, or merely to explain himself in some material part of his speech; or to the manner or words of the question, keeping himself to that only and not traveling into the merits of it; or to the orders of the House, if they be transgressed, keeping within that line, and falling into the matter itself.

---

* The presiding officer should give the floor to the member whose voice he first hears. Where the sense of the House is taken on the question as to which member was first up, it is taken first on the member announced by the presiding officer. The legislative assemblies of this country frequently provide by special rule that the decision of the Chair in cases aforesaid shall be final.

But if the Speaker rises to speak, the member standing up ought to sit down, that he may be first heard. Nevertheless, though the Speaker may of right speak to matters of order, and be first heard, he is restrained from speaking on any other subject except when the House have occasion for facts within his knowledge; then he may, with their leave, state the matter of fact.*

No member is to speak impertinently, superfluously or tediously, or depart from the question pending; nor use indecent language against the proceedings of the House; no prior determination of which is to be reflected on by any member, unless he intends to conclude with a motion to rescind it. But while a proposition under consideration is undetermined, though it has even been reported by a committee,

---

* According to usage in this country the presiding officer in legislative assemblies and all other deliberative bodies, where he is a member of the same, may participate in debate and other proceedings the same as other members; but for this purpose he should call some member to the Chair and take his place on the floor of the assembly.

reflections on it are no reflections on the House.

No member in speaking is to mention another member then present by his name; but should describe him by his seat in the House, or as the member who spoke last, or on the other side of the question, and the like;* nor is he to digress from the matter pending, to indulge in personal reflections upon another member, by reviling him or speaking unmannerly words against a particular member. The consequence of a measure may be reprobated in strong terms; but to arraign the motives of those who propose or advocate it, is a personality and against order.

No member is to disturb another in his speech by hissing, coughing or spitting; nor stand up to interrupt him; nor pass between the Speaker and the member speaking; nor go across or walk up and down the room; or take books or papers from the table, or engage in writing there.

---

* In deliberative assemblies in this country members in debate are referred to as "the gentleman from," (naming the district he represents.)

Nevertheless, if a member finds it is not the inclination of the House to hear him, and that, by conversation or any other noise they endeavor to drown his voice, it is the most prudent way to submit to the pleasure of the House, and sit down, for it scarcely ever happens that members are inclined to ill manners of this kind without sufficient reason. Members are not apt to be inattentive to a member who says anything worth their hearing.

In case of disorder if repeated calls do not produce order, the Speaker may call by his name any member obstinately persisting in irregularity, whereupon the House may require the member to withdraw. He is then to be heard in exculpation and to withdraw. Then the Speaker states the offense committed and the House considers the degree of punishment they will inflict.*

Disorderly words on the part of a member are not to be noticed until he has

---

\* In case of disorderly conduct on the part of members assuming the nature of an affray, the assembly should at once be adjourned until order can be restored.

finished his speech. Then the person objecting to them, and desiring them to be taken down by the clerk at the table, must repeat them. The Speaker may then direct the clerk to take them down in his minutes. But if he thinks them not disorderly he may delay the direction. If the call becomes pretty general, he orders the clerk to take them down, as stated by the objecting member. They are then a part of his minutes and when read to the offending member, he may deny they were his words, and the House must then decide by a question whether they are his words or not. Then the member may justify them or explain the sense in which he used them, or apologize.*

If the House is satisfied, no further proceeding is necessary. But if two members still insist to take the sense of the House the member complained of must withdraw before that question is stated, and then the sense of the House is to be taken. When any member has spoken, or other

---

*In parliament to speak irreverently or seditiously against the King is against order. 2 Hatsell, 170.

business intervened after offensive words spoken, they cannot be taken notice of for censure. And this is for the common security of all and to prevent mistakes which must happen if words are not taken down immediately.*

Disorderly words spoken in a committee must be written down as in the House; but the committee can only report them to the House for action.

It is a breach of order in debate to notice what has been said on the same subject in the other House, or the particular votes or majorities on it there; because the opinion of each House should be left to its own independency, not to be influenced by the proceedings of the other; and the quoting of them might give rise to reflections leading to a misunderstanding between the two Houses. Neither House can exercise any authority over a member or officer of the other, but should complain to the House of which he is a member or officer, and leave the punishment to them.

---

* Formerly disorderly words might be taken down at any time the same day. 2 Hatsell, 196.

No member may be present when a bill, or any business concerning himself is being debated; nor is any member to speak to the merits of it until such interested member withdraws. The rule is that if a charge against a member arises out of a report of a committee, or examination of witnesses in the House, as the member knows from that to what points he is to direct his exculpation, he may be heard to those points before any question is moved or stated against him. He is then to be heard and withdraw before any question is moved. But if the question itself is the charge, as for breach of order, or matter arising in debate, then the matter must be stated, that is, the question must be moved, himself heard, and then to withdraw.

Where the private interests of a member are concerned in a bill or question he is to withdraw. The rule does not admit of his taking part on a question in which he is interested. In a case so contrary not only to the laws of decency, but to the fundamental principles of the social compact, which denies to any man to be a judge in his own cause, it is for the honor of the House that this rule of immemorial observance should be strictly adhered to.*

When a question of order arises in the course of debate, or indeed at any other time in the proceedings of the House, it may be adjourned to give time to look into precedents on the subject.

## Questions not Debatable.

In the preceding remarks referring to the various classes of motions or questions arising in deliberative assemblies, mention has been incidentally made of those which are not debatable. The purpose here is to group all such motions together under one head, for purpose of convenience of reference, adding some general remarks on the subject. By the general rules of parliamentary law the questions not debatable are:

A motion to adjourn.
A motion to lie on the table.

---

* 2 Hatsell, 119, 121.  6 Grey, 368.

A motion for the previous question.

A motion for indefinite postponement.

A motion to read a paper or document pending a question.

A motion to take up particular items of business, or relating to priority of business.

As a general rule all questions of privilege are not debatable.

So incidental questions are in general not debatable. But an amendment to an amendment, which is classed as an incidental question, may be debated.

A motion to postpone to a time fixed beyond that of the final adjournment of the assembly is equivalent to indefinite postponement, and, therefore, for the like reason is rot debatable; otherwise the motion to postpone to a time certain is debatable; so a motion to adjourn to a time fixed is debatable. And a motion to lie on the table if limited or qualified in any way would thereby become debatable.

It is not the policy of parliamentary law to encourage debate or delay in the proceedings of a deliberative assembly, which has given rise to motions through which debate on a question may be terminated or restrained. Debate is expected to be directed to the main question, so where debate is allowed on a subsidiary or other motion, it proceeds rather on the theory that it has some direct bearing on the main subject, or that the principal subject is in some way brought in question.

Speakers in Congress have decided, and the decisions have been sustained by the House, that inasmuch as the motion to lie on the table is not debatable, so the motion to *reconsider* must be taken without debate.\*

But as we have seen such is not the uniform rule in legislative or deliberative assemblies.† But in adopting the rule allowing debate on a motion to reconsider it would seem as if the debate should be confined as much as possible to the reasons for or against reconsideration. This it is true may to a certain extent, incidentally reach the merits of the question.

---

\* Matthias' Manual, 92.    † See ante p. 67.

## "The Casting Vote."

By the Constitution of the United States the Vice President is President of the Senate, but it is provided that he shall have no vote, unless the Senate is equally divided.* The like provision exists in regard to Lieut. Governor in the several States of the Union. In cities and other municipal corporations of this kind, in many instances, the Mayor or principal officer of the corporation is made presiding officer of the city or corporation council; but not being a member of the council, provision is made that he shall have no vote, unless where the council is equally divided. This, in common speech, is called *the casting vote.*

But in all deliberative assemblies like the House of Representatives in Congress, the popular branch of the legislative assemblies of the several States, mass meetings of the people, meetings of societies and the like, where the presiding officer is chosen from the assembly or meeting, and

---

* Const. U. S., Art. 1, Sec. 3.

thus constituting one of their number, the presiding officer has a vote on all questions the same as any other member. But in case of a *tie vote* so called, or in case where the members are equally divided, in the absence of any rule of the assembly, or provision of the Constitution or Statute to the contrary, the pending measure would be lost.

## "The Enacting Clause."

In the early history of legislation in the English parliament we are informed that acts of parliament were in general passed in aid of or to cure defects in the common law. And the early custom in preparing bills for acts was to commence with a preamble reciting the defects in the law complained of, or whatever else seemed required, and to conclude with a provision as circumstances demanded. This provision would, as a general thing, be very short and comprised in a single clause; hence it was called the *enacting clause* to distinguish it from the preamble of the bill, so that a bill for an act of parliament was composed of two parts, *the preamble* and the *enacting clause*. It was called the *enacting clause* because its office or functions were to declare or create the law. In common speech it was referred to simply as *the clause*.

Gurdon in his history of the high court of parliament, published in 1731, in referring to an act of parliament passed in the reign of Richard II, says: "To save the reader the trouble of having recourse to the act of parliament I transcribe the enacting clause of the statute of Richard II: "If any person of the Realm having "summons to parliament," etc. Here follows the provision of the act in twelve lines only comprised in a single *clause*.

In time, however, as will be noticed by reference to the English statutes, the provisions of acts of parliament became drawn out into several clauses or sections so that the term *clause* was no longer applicable, whereupon this portion of the act became known as the *enacting words*.

From the earliest time we find that in

framing or enacting laws certain forms of words were used preceding the enacting clause, called the *style* of the act; the office thereof being to show by what authority the statute is enacted. Thus in the reign of Henry VII, says the writer before mentioned:* "The style of Acts of Parliament in Henry VII's time, is by the assent of the Lords, spiritual and temporal, and Commons in Parliament assembled," etc. So that we have in an act of parliament the preamble, the style, and the *enacting clause*, which latter part, as we have seen, later on became referred to as the *enacting words*.

The Constitution of Illinois declares that "The *style* of all laws of this State shall be: Be it enacted by the People of the State of Illinois, represented in the General Assembly."† And a similar provision prescribing the style of laws exists in most other States of the Union, which seems to have been borrowed from the English precedent in regard to statute laws.

---

\* 2 Gurdon's Hist. of Parliament.
† Const. Ill. Art. 4, Sec. 11.

It seems that in practice in the English parliament a very effectual and convenient motion became adapted for rejecting bills where their provisions were not favorably received; that of a motion to strike out the enacting clause, which if no further action was taken was a rejection or defeat of the bill.

Some law writers of the present day in referring to our statutes speak of the *style* of acts of the Legislature as the *enacting clause* or *enacting words*, while from the earliest time these words, *Be it enacted, etc.*, or those performing the like office, have been known as the *style* of the laws, and to refer to them as *the enacting clause* cannot be regarded otherwise than an unpardonable misnomer. In some legislative assemblies in this country where the motion to strike out the *enacting words* or *enacting clause* of bills has been adopted, the same erroneous misapplication of terms is practiced.

In practice it becomes material as to whether a motion of this kind is to be applied to the mere *style* of the bill, or the enacting words which follow it; for the effect of such a motion being carried in the affirmative would be widely different in either case.* The fact is the *style* of the bill being added to laws by force of the Constitution, a motion to strike it out of a bill would not strictly be in order and ought not to be entertained.

If it is understood that a motion to strike out the enacting words or clause, if carried in the affirmative, removes the *style* from the bill, no effect whatever is in reality produced thereby. The bill itself is still pending before the assembly, and may, nevertheless, be advanced to its final consideration. The *style* is a formality which may be added even at the time the bill is engrossed. The better practice at this day of voluminous bills would be to change the form of this motion to a motion to strike out all after the style of the bill. Indeed, in some legislative

---

\* For after the enacting words following the style of the bill are stricken out, it would still be in order, in the absence of any special rule to the contrary to move to insert other words in their stead.

assemblies this form of motion has been adopted.*

## USE OF THE GAVEL.

At this day a gavel or small mallet is used by the presiding officer in legislative bodies and other deliberative assemblies. The use of this implement in such assemblies appears to be of modern custom, which seems to have had its origin in Masonic lodges, wherein it came into use by the master or presiding officer, borrowed from operative masonry as in the case of all other emblems used also in speculative free masonry. This implement was originally made use of by operative masons to break off the rough corners of stones the better to fit them for the builders' use.

---

* The error of calling the style of laws the *enacting clause* seems to come from the suggestive fact that the word *enact* occurs therein, and it may be answered that it is immaterial what name we apply to an object so long as the intention is understood. Conceding this to be so, still the point in this case is that the motion to strike out the style of the bill by any name whatever is improper, and unknown to parliamentary law.

In forming lodges in speculative masonry the gavel, called in masonry "the common gavel," or "stone hammer," seems to have been naturally suggested as a proper implement to be used by the master in performing the functions or duties of his station while presiding over his lodge.

In speculative masonry, so-called, the common gavel is adopted as an emblem of authority, and as such it has a language by custom accompanying its use to the effect following:

*One* rap calls the lodge to order and calls up any member addressed by the master. *Two* raps calls up the officers of the lodge. *Three* raps calls up all the members and *one* rap seats them.

It would seem, therefore, that legislative and other deliberative assemblies in borrowing this implement from the source mentioned, should, as far as the same can be adopted to such occasions, take with it and use the language attending it as the same has been employed time out of mind.

In the use of the gavel in deliberative assemblies one **rap** will call the assembly to order, and indicate that members are requested to be seated. In requesting members to rise on any occasion as in case of prayer by the chaplain, in imitating the custom in masonic lodges, three raps would suffice for that purpose, following which one rap would seat them.

In calling the assembly to order only one rap of the gavel should be given. It frequently occurs that a person is chosen presiding officer who, not having given attention to the proper use of the gavel, uses it indiscriminately according to his own notions of its proper use; in such cases in calling the assembly to order the chances are that he will start out with three loud distinct raps, having the idea that the more raps he gives the more effectual is his effort to command attention. This is an inexcusable error in the use of the gavel.

It is noticed that presiding officers frequently fall into another error in the use of the gavel, which is not only in bad taste, but may be carried to that extent as to be exceedingly annoying and will entirely fail of the object sought: Where noise and confusion occurs in the assembly in commanding silence, he himself partaking of the excitement of the occasion, commences to rap with his gavel with great force upon the desk before him, repeating and continuing the same as if pounding stone or driving an obstinate nail until order is finally restored.

When noise or confusion occurs in a deliberative assembly to such extent as to require the attention or interference of the presiding officer for its suppression, the more proper course on his part is to reverse his gavel, employing the handle and giving with the same a rapid succession of raps on his desk sufficient to attract attention, and thereupon request silence. If such course will not restore order, it is certain that the use of the gavel in any more demonstrative manner will fail of that end.

According to the general rule in conducting the proceedings of the assembly in good taste on the part of the presiding officer, one rap of the gavel is all that is required on any occasion, and while one rap will call the assembly to order, the same will be proper to announce that any particular order of business is closed, or for commanding the attention of members for any purpose, and one rap should be given when declaring the assembly adjourned. Indeed, in conducting the proceedings of deliberative assemblies there would seem to be no instance in the proper use of the gavel adapted to such occasions where more than one rap would be proper or in good taste.

Another rule should be observed by the presiding officer in conducting the proceedings of the assembly on his part in good taste. Having called the assembly to order, the better course is to drop the gavel upon his desk, there to remain until occasion calls for its proper use. Presiding officers frequently fall into the habit of holding the gavel constantly in their hands, and in recognizing a member who rises to address the chair, they throw out the head of the gavel towards him with force as if to strike him a blow. This is a habit which should be avoided. It is not intended that the gavel should be used for any such purpose. The presiding officer in recognizing a member who rises to address the chair, if he desires any particular demonstration on his part aside from the general rule to indicate to a member that he is recognized,* may manifest the same by a waive of the hand in the direction of the member. Nothing further would seem to be necessary.

## Deportment of Members.

In legislative assemblies the deportment of members, and courtesy among themselves during their official intercourse, is a matter justly claiming attention.

There are in every-day life certain rules of deportment on the part of individuals incident to good breeding, which every one is expected to observe, all tending towards good order and a more finished state of society. So in legislative assem-

---

*See ante page 43.

blies, there are, or should be, certain rules of decorum or standard of deportment attended by a degree of courtesy between members which all are expected to observe as a mark of respect on official occasions of this importance.

It should be borne in mind that occasions of this kind are not in the nature of social gatherings for personal amusement or individual gratification, in which members are at liberty to adopt or disregard rules as may seem best in rendering the occasion most enjoyable to themselves, but is one strictly of official character, in which no member has any private concern. Nor is he at liberty to indulge in such conduct as might be permitted in gatherings of individuals for mere social purposes. The conduct of members is expected to be such as will constantly impress upon the mind the importance of the occasion and the responsibility resting upon each.

The association of members being for official purposes, their deportment and bearing towards each other should be regulated accordingly, and that which might be proper, or at least not objectionable in a gathering for mere social purposes, might be highly improper in an assembly of this kind convened for official purposes.

In social intercourse between persons of intimate acquaintance, in addressing each other, familiarity is not only not improper, but indeed to a certain extent at least, is expected, while in a legislative assembly between members the same degree of familiarity would in general be a breach of good rules. For instance in such assemblies members in their intercourse as such are expeceed to address each other as "Mr."

The appellation of "Joe," "Jack" or "Jim" may not be objectionable in social intercourse among intimate friends under certain circumstances, but among members of a legislative assembly this would be a breach of etiquette which ought not to be indulged in at any time, whether it be while engaged in the line of official duty or on other occasions during the time their relation as members continues to exist.

It is said of Henry Clay, whose own personal deportment was that of a polished gentleman, that while Speaker of the house of representatives in Congress, his aim was to enforce strictly all rules of order as to conduct of members, in which he went to the fullest extent, even whenever he observed a member who in disregard of proper decorum was noticed with his feet upon the desk or table in front of him—a boorish habit sometimes indulged in, he always took occasion in some manner least offensive to promptly call him to order.

So there are certain rules of conduct among members, requiring of them, at least whilst their official relations exist, that they refrain from speaking ill of each other, and forbear to indulge in unjust criticisms on the course or conduct of fellow members; and this as well in debate as on other occasions. The public interests are supposed to be jeopardized to the extent that bitterness of feeling among members is allowed to be engendered.

## Peculiarities of Legislation in Parliament.

In the British Parliament the bills are engrossed on one or more long rolls of parchment, sewed together. When a bill is amended on third reading, if a new clause is added, it is done by tacking a separate piece of parchment on the bill, which is called a *rider*.

In the House of Commons, the members vote "aye" or "no." In the House of Peers, they answer "content," or "not content."

The King's answer to the bills presented to him for his approbation, is announced to the House by the clerk in Norman French. If the King consents to a public bill, the clerk says *Le roy le veut,* (the King wills it so to be;) if to a private bill, *Soit fait comme il est desire,* (be it as it is desired.) If the King refuses his consent, it is in the gentle language of *Le roy s'avisera,* (the King will advise upon it.)

The title Speaker is given to the presiding officer of the House of Commons, because he alone has the right to speak to or address the King, in the name and in behalf of the house.* His salary and perquisites amount to about £8,000 per annum.

When the House of Commons divides, in order to take a vote, one party goes out, and the other remains in the room. This has made it important which go forth first and which remain, because the latter secure the votes of all the indolent, the indifferent, and the inattentive. Their general rule, therefore, is that those who give their vote for the preservation of the orders of the House, stay in. The one party being gone forth, the Speaker names two tellers from the affirmative, and two from the negative side, who first count those sitting in the House and report the number to the Speaker. They then place themselves within the door two on each side, and count those who went forth, as they come in, and report the number to the Speaker.

---

* See ante, p. 30.

## Language of Parliamentary Law.

As a general rule every trade, occupation and profession, has a language or class of terms peculiar to itself, growing out of attending circumstances and conditions; so it is with Parliamentary Law; and not only this, but the rule in this regard is held by good parliamentarians to the utmost strictness

The lawyer in discussing his case before the Court is expected to use terms belonging to his profession, and his learning as a lawyer and familiarity with rules of law will be marked in a greater or less degree, according to his observance of terms, recognized as belonging to the profession. So a good parliamentarian will be found using those terms, which have been settled time out of mind, as applicable in deliberative assemblies. Any neglect in this regard by members of a deliberative assembly, or misapplication of terms will be taken as evidence of the want of a proper appreciation of the rules of parliamentary law.

For instance, in Legislative Assemblies

we hear members thoughtlessly using the expression: "The bill was killed." Farmers tell us about killing their hogs, and in their occupation it is not an inappropriate term to apply in such cases, but an expression of this kind concerning proceedings in a legislative assembly is, to say the least, far from being appropriate.

A bill for an act in a legislative assembly which fails to pass on the question of its passage being taken, in proper terms is said to be *lost*, or *it has failed to pass*, or *the bill was defeated*. In bringing measures before a legislative assembly, the three customary modes are as follows: by petition, by resolution, or by bill. In proper speech petitions are *presented*, resolutions are *offered*, and bills are *introduced*; to say that a bill or resolution was *presented* is not a proper expression in parliamentary proceedings.

Good parliamentarians adhere strictly to the foregoing terms with reference to petitions, resolutions and bills. And in debate we say in referring to measures of the kind pending " the petition *presented* by the gentleman from A."; "the resolutions *offered* by the gentleman from B."; "the bill *introduced* by the gentleman from C."

In legislative assemblies bills undergo three several readings, styled the first, second and third reading, each of which comes in a separate order of business. In referring to bills in these several stages they are designated by the *reading* in which they lie, and on taking up bills on these several readings, the term would be: consideration of bills on *first* reading, consideration of bills on *second* reading, consideration of bills on *third* reading; after a bill has been read the third time, the question recurs on the passage of the bill, which is put by the presiding officer in this manner: "Shall the bill pass?" Hence has arisen an erroneous practice with members when referring to bills on third reading of saying, *bills on their passage.* This literally taken would imply an obligation on the part of the assembly to pass the bill; this is an inappropiate term; the proper parliamentary expression in such cases is, *consideration of bills on third reading.*

A motion that the House proceed to the *passage* of bills, would be grossly inappropriate; the motion should be that the House do now proceed to the consideration of bill on third reading. And as before stated after a bill has been read the third time, the question will recurr without any motion whatever on the passage of the bill, that is, the pending question will be " shall the bill pass," as before remarked.

## Parliamentary Law in Secret Societies.

There are classes of societies in existence at this day which are called Secret Societies, from the fact that their meetings are open to those only who are members; going upon the principle that no one but their members have any concern in their affairs.

The oldest of these is the Masonic order or order of Free Masonry which is traced by some to the building of Solomon's temple, and it is said the architects from the African coast, Mahometans, brought it into Spain about the sixth century as a protection against Christian fanatics. Its introduction into Great Britain has been fixed at the year A. D. 674, although by other authorities it is assigned a much earlier date. The grand lodge at York was founded A. D. 926. Free Masonry was interdicted in England A. D. 1424, but it afterward rose into great repute. In 1717 the grand lodge of England was established; that of Ireland was established in 1739, and that of Scotland in 1736.

Next came the order of Odd Fellows, which had its rise in England during the past century, and which like other secret societies that have followed are to a greater or less extent in imitation of Masonry.

These societies in general, conduct their proceedings in the manner of deliberative assemblies; hence, the rules of parliamentary law are to a certain extent applicable in conducting the same, qualified or restricted according to their constitutions and by-laws, or ancient rules and usages.

In the Masonic lodge, the master or presiding officer, so far as the ancient landmarks so called are concerned, possesses absolute or supreme authority and is not in general obliged to recognize in this respect rules of parliamentary law.

But in all those matters which relate to the financial or mere business affairs of the lodge, it is intended that the brethren or members shall have an equal voice. In such cases it would follow that the rules of parliamentary law governing deliberative assemblies should be observed.

One of the essentials in societies of this kind, is harmony among its members. This being so, it would follow that such rules should be observed in conducting their proceedings as will tend to that end. From which the policy would be to disregard many of those dilatory motions that have been introduced into parliamentary law, and which tend to delay, hinder or obstruct proceedings, whereby advantage may be derived on mere technicalities and through which discussion might be prolonged and bad feeling engendered.

In proceedings in a Masonic lodge there is no such thing as privileged questions as understood in parliamentary law; such questions would be inconsistent with the power which the ancient landmarks have reposed in the master of the lodge, so in a Masonic lodge there is no such motion as a motion to adjourn; questions of this kind being regulated by the ancient constitutions of the order, so there would probably be no such motion as a motion to lay on the table; in its stead, however, may be adopted a motion serving the like or even a better purpose, that of a motion to postpone, which if it related to the mere business affairs of the lodge would be proper.

A motion to refer a principal proposition would also be proper; but a demand for the previous question would be inconsistent, for the power vested in the master by the ancient constitutions would authorize him in his discretion to order that which would be accomplished by a call for the previous question.

All that which is regulated in the Masonic order by its ancient constitutions or landmarks so called, is excluded from the operation of parliamentary law. Questions arising in such cases are submitted by the master of the lodge to the members merely to aid him in the performance of his duties, or the exercise of his discretion through such advice as he may thereby obtain from them.

# Summary of General Rules.

### PARLIAMENTARY LAW.

1. Parliamentary law consists of rules which are recognized as governing proceedings in deliberative assemblies.

2. It is so called from the rules of order existing from long established usage in the British parliament.

3. By custom the general rules of parliamentary law apply in all deliberative assemblies without the necessity of being formally adopted.

### DELIBERATIVE ASSEMBLIES.

1. A deliberative assembly is a congregation of people or convention of persons for the consideration of matters in which all are concerned, or in which all have an equal voice.

2. A small number of persons forming a mere executive board is not considered strictly a deliberative assembly, to which the rules of parliamentary law are necessarily applicable to any general extent.

3. A deliberative assembly can not proceed to business until properly organized.

## OFFICERS.

1. A deliberative assembly is not properly orga ized until officers are chosen and installed.

2. The officers necessary are a president or chairman and secretary or clerk; other officers may be added as circumstances may dictate.

3. The chairman or president presides, and the secretary or clerk records the proceedings of the assembly.

## QUORUM.

1. A quorum is a majority of the members of the assembly.

2 The business of an assembly can not properly proceed unless a quorum is present.

3. The number constituting a quorum may be otherwise fixed by the rules of the assembly.

4. All questions are determined by a majority vote of the members present constituting a quorum.

## MANNER OF PRESENTING BUSINESS.

1. Every member of a deliberative assembly has the right to present propositions for the action of the assembly.

2. Business is generally introduced by a motion.

3. A motion is a verbal or oral proposition of a member.

4. Propositions may also be submitted by a committee, which is called their report.

5. Propositions offered by members, except mere motions in the progress of proceeding, should be reduced to writing and may be required to be put in writing on demand of a member.

6. A proposition when reduced to writing is generally in the form of a resolution, commencing with the word "Resolved."

7. Subjects for action may be set in motion also by a communication to the assembly.

8. Communications for this purpose are of two kinds: First, for information of the assembly in matters of fact called a memorial; second, those which contain a request for some action on the part of the assembly called a petition.

9. The technical difference between a memorial and a petition is, that the former is a mere representation of existing facts whilst the latter is a request that something be done.

10. In presenting a petition the custom is for the member presenting it to state the substance of the same, describing it as the petition of——, naming the person first sign-

ing it and the number of other signers, thus: "The petition of A. B. and one hundred other signers," or as the case may be.

11. When a petition is presented the custom is to receive it as a matter of course without any formal motion to that effect.

12. In general no proposition or question can be acted upon except on motion or at the instance of a member.

13. In case of a resolution offered by a member or report from a committee the question recurs upon concurring in the same without the necessity of a formal motion to that effect.

14. The offering of a resolution by a member or submitting a report by a committee carries with it or implies a motion that the same be adopted or concurred in.

15. No member is entitled to make a motion or present a proposition until he has obtained the floor for that purpose.

16. The manner of obtaining the floor is for a member to rise in his place and address the presiding officer by his title; on being recognized he has obtained the floor and is entitled to proceed.

17. A motion is not before the assembly for consideration until stated by the presiding officer.

18. Where a motion or proposition is in writing it is not properly before the assembly until it has been read.

19. When a proposition is offered or a motion is made and seconded it becomes the property of the assembly, and can not be withdrawn or modified by the mover except by leave of the assembly on motion or by general consent.

20. The presiding officer should rise to put motions or state questions for consideration.

21. After a vote has been taken on a question and the result declared by the presiding officer it becomes final, subject to reconsideration in certain cases.

22. If any member doubts the result of the vote when taken *viva voce*, before the result is declared he may call for a division of the house.

23. A division of the house on any question, is by those in the affirmative rising and being counted, then by those in the negative rising and being counted.

24. If any member doubts the result of the vote by dividing the house, he may call for tellers to ascertain and report the vote taken by them.

25. In appointing tellers it is customary to appoint one person from the affirmative,

and another person from the negative side of the question.

26. When a division of the house is desired or tellers are demanded, it must be called for before the result has been finally declared by the presiding officer.

## Motions in General.

### DIFFERENT KINDS OF MOTIONS.

1. There is presumed to be always pending a principal motion or main question.

2. When a proposition is made it is usually called a *motion*; when it is stated to the assembly by the presiding officer for consideration it is called a *question*, and if adopted it becomes the *order, resolution* or *vote* of the assembly.

3. Motions or questions aside from the principal motion in a deliberative assembly are: 1. Subsidiary motions. 2. Privileged questions. 3. Incidental questions or motions.

*First: Subsidiary motions* in common use are, 1. To lie on the table. 2. The previous question. 3. Postponement, either indefinite or to a time certain. 4. Commitment. 5. Amendment.

*Second: Privileged questions* or motions

## Summary of General Rules. 127

are, 1. Motions to adjourn. 2. Motions or questions relating to rights and privileges of the assembly or to its members individually. 3. Motions for the orders of the day.

*Third:* *Incidental questions* are, 1. Questions of order. 2. Motions for the reading of papers, etc. 3. Leave to withdraw a motion. 4. Suspension of a rule. 5. Amendment of an amendment.

### PRINCIPAL MOTIONS.

1. A principal motion is a proposition embracing some principle or asserting some fact brought before the assembly for consideration.

### SUBSIDIARY QUESTIONS.

1. Subsidiary questions or motions are those which relate to a principal motion and are made use of to enable the assembly to dispose of the main or principal question in a particular way, as indicated by this class of questions.

2. Subsidiary questions, unlike priviledged and incidental questions, can only be pending or moved when there is a principal question pending to which they may be applied.

3. Subsidiary questions are dilatory in their nature, as they are intended, in the absence of special rules to the contrary, to

interrupt or prevent a direct vote on the main question, and dispose of it in some other manner.

### PRIVILEGED QUESTIONS.

4. Privileged questions or motions are in general independent questions, having no reference to the main question, but which may be pending while the main proposition and subsidiary motions thereto are pending.

### INCIDENTAL QUESTIONS.

1. Incidental questions are in general such as arise out of other questions, and are to be decided before those which give rise to them.

## Motions and Manner of Proceeding.

### GENERAL RULES.

1. A motion is simply a proposition of a member as his individual sentiments, which he desires the assembly to adopt.

2. Where a proposition offered is adopted, it becomes the conclusion or sense of the assembly.

3. A proposition by a single member is not considered as sufficient to claim attention; it is therefore required that it should

be approved or seconded by one other member.

4. When a motion is seconded, the mover is entitled to have it put or disposed of by the assembly.

5. The mode of seconding a motion is by some member other than the one who offers it, announcing his approval of the same by saying that he seconds the motion.

6. All motions are presumed to be seconded, unless the point is made and the contrary is shown.

7. In good practice a presiding officer does not pause to inquire if a motion is seconded; he will presume that it is seconded and proceed to put the motion, unless the contrary is made to appear.

8. It is not in order for a member when he obtains the floor and makes a principal motion, to follow it up at the same time with a subsidiary or other motion relating to it, as a motion that it lie on the table.

9. Where it is desired to delay or postpone a proposition for further information or reflection and examination, the usual motions under such circumstances are *postponement to some future day or time*, and to *lie on the table*.

10. Where it is desired to suppress a proposition for a time, or altogether, the motions

for this purpose are *the previous question* and *indefinite postponement.*

11. Where it is desired to inquire into or perfect a proposition, the proper course is to *refer it to a committee,* called a motion to commit.

12. Where the general features of a proposition are acceptable, but alterations in some particular are desired, the motion for that purpose is a motion *to amend.*

### SUBSIDIARY MOTIONS.

#### 1. *Lie on the Table.*

1. Where a proposition is laid on the table its consideration can not be resumed without a vote to that effect.

2. A motion to lie on the table is not debatable nor susceptible of amendment.

It takes precedence and supersedes all other subsidiary motions.

A vote to lay a proposition on the table can not be reconsidered.

3. Where a proposition is ordered to lie on the table, it is removed from before the assembly until taken up by vote.

4. A proposition which has been laid on the table may be taken up any time for consideration, by a vote of the assembly.

5. A motion to take a proposition from the table is not a privileged motion, so it can

not be properly entertained while some particular order of business, or some other particular motion is pending.

6. As a motion to lie on the table is not debatable, so a motion to take a measure from the table is not debatable.

7. A motion to take a measure from the table is in the nature of a principal proposition, and if the motion is lost the vote by which it is lost may be reconsidered.

### 2. *The Previous Question.*

1. Where a member desires a vote to be taken on a proposition without further debate or delay he may move the previous question.

2. The form of putting the motion for the previous question is: "The previous question is moved, shall the main question be now put?"

3. When a motion for the previous question is sustained whereby the main question is ordered, the main question is the original proposition with pending amendments, if any, each of which is to be disposed of in its proper order.

4. The previous question stands on equal degree with all other subsidiary motions, except the motion to lie on the table.

### 3. *Postponement.*

1. A motion to postpone indefinitely is to be decided without debate.

2. Where a motion to postpone indefinitely is decided in the affirmative it removes the question before the assembly.

3. A motion to postpone to a day beyond the sitting of the assembly is of the same effect as indefinite postponement.

4. When a motion is postponed to a time fixed, when that time arrives it will be in order to resume its consideration.

5. A motion to postpone is either indefinite, or to a time certain. In both cases it may be amended; in the former by fixing the time, in the latter by substituting one time for another. The latter is treated like filling blanks.

### 4. *Motion to Commit.*

1. A motion to refer a proposition to a select committee and a standing committee may be made and pending at the same time. The latter motion takes precedence and should be first put.

2. A part or the whole of any subject may be referred to a committee, or portions may be referred to several different committees.

3. After a motion to commit a proposition

a motion to amend the proposition is not in order.

4. A motion to commit may itself be amended by substituting another committee from that named in the motion, or by enlarging or diminishing the number of the committee when the motion is to refer to a select committee.

5. When a motion to commit is made, it may also be moved that the committee be instructed as to their action upon the proposition.

6. When a motion to commit is carried the effect is to remove the subject involved from before the assembly for the time being.

7. A motion to commit stands in the same degree with the previous question and postponement, but it takes precedence of a motion to amend.

### 5. *Amendment.*

1. Amending a proposition is either by adding words or taking words from it, or by transposition of words, or by division of a subject, which is accomplished under different modes, which may be classified thus: 1. Filling blanks; 2. Striking out; 3. By inserting; 4. Striking out and inserting; 5. Division of a proposition.

2. A motion to amend stands in the same

degree only with the previous question and indefinite postponement; neither, if first moved, is superseded by the other. It is liable to be superseded by a motion to postpone to a certain day and may be superseded by a motion to commit.

1. *Filling Blanks.* Filling blanks in a proposition is in the nature of an original motion, to be made and decided before the principal question.

2. In case of filling blanks with time and number, motions may be made for that purpose, and the motion taken on each by itself. Several motions for this purpose may be made and pending before any of them are put to the question.

3. In filling blanks, the usual rule is to take the question first on the highest number, the largest sum, and the longest time, to which rule, however, there are some exceptions.

1. *Striking Out.* If an amendment is proposed by striking out, and it is rejected, it can not be again moved to strike out the same words, nor a part of them; but it may be moved to strike out the same words with others, or a part of the same words with others.

1. *Amendment by Inserting.* If an amend-

ment is proposed by inserting or adding a paragraph or words, and it is rejected, it can not be again moved to insert the same words or part of them.

2. Where an amendment is proposed by adding a paragraph or words, and rejected, it may be again moved to insert the same with others, or a part of the same words or paragraph with others, if the coherence makes them different propositions.

1. *Striking Out and Inserting.* A motion to strike out and insert may be divided by a vote of the assembly and each put separately.

2. When a proposition to strike out and insert is divided, the question is first to be taken on striking out. On a motion to strike out and insert the manner of stating the question is first to read the whole passage to be amended, as it stands, then the words proposed to be struck out; next those to be inserted; and lastly the whole passage as it stands when amended.

1. *Division of a Proposition.* Where a proposition is composed of two or more whole parts which are susceptible of division into several parts, it may be divided by order of the assembly on motion, as in other cases.

2. Where a proposition is divided, the question divided takes a series of indepen-

dent propositions. This may be done by order of the assembly on demand of a member.

3. On demand or motion for division of a proposition, the presiding officer puts the question before the assembly for its decision, as in other cases.

4. The presiding officer may decide whether the proposition is susceptible of division and how many parts it may be divided into, subject to appeal, as in other cases.

### PRIVILEGED QUESTIONS.

1. Privileged questions are: 1. Motion to adjourn; 2. Motions or questions relating to the rights and privileges of the assembly, or of its members individually; 3. Motions for the orders of the day.

#### 1. *Adjournment.*

1. A motion to adjourn supersedes all other questions. It is not debatable and generally can not be amended.

2. A motion to adjourn to a time fixed can be amended by offering some other time, and is debatable.

3. An adjournment for a short time on the same day is called a recess.

4. Whilst the general rule relating to a motion to adjourn is stated to be that it is

always in order, yet when put and carried in the negative it can not be again put a second time in succession unless some intervening motion or proposition has been entertained and acted upon by the assembly.

5. Nor can a privileged motion of this kind be moved by any member while another member has the floor.

6. An adjournment without fixing a day or time on which the assembly shall again meet is equivalent to a dissolution of the assembly.

7. When an assembly adjourns while a question is pending the question is removed from further consideration, and will not be pending in the assembly at the time to which it adjourned.

8. A motion to adjourn is not debatable and can not be amended, nor can a vote thereon be reconsidered.

2. *Questions of Privilege.*

1. Questions of privilege are such as concern the rights and privileges of the assembly or individual members, as when the proceedings are disturbed or interrupted by strangers or members or where a quarrel arises between individual members and the like. Questions of privilege take precedence of all others except that of adjournment.

2. Questions of privilege supersede for the time being the pending question together with all subsidiary and incidental questions, and must be first disposed of.

3. When a question of privilege is settled the question interupted by it is to be resumed at the point at which it was suspended.

### 3. *Orders of the Day.*

1. When the consideration of a subject is assigned for a particular day the matter so assigned is called the order of the day.

2. Where there are several subjects assigned for the same day they are called the orders of the day.

3. Where a question is made the subject of an order for consideration on a particular day, it thereby becomes the privileged question for that day.

4. A motion for the orders of the day supersedes all other motions except questions of privilege and motion to adjourn even though a member has the floor.

5. But to entitle this motion to supersede the questions as aforesaid it must be for the orders generally if there be more than one, and not for any particular one.

6. If decided in the affirmative the orders are then proceeded with in the order in which they stand.

7. Where an order is assigned for any particular hour of the day, a motion to proceed to it is not a privileged motion until that hour has arrived, but if no time is fixed the order is for the entire day and every part of it.

8. Where there are several orders of the day and one is fixed for a particular hour, if the others are taken up before that hour, they are to be proceeded with as they stand until that hour, and then the subject assigned for that hour is to be next in order.

9. Where a motion for the orders of the day is decided in the affirmative, the question pending at the time is removed from before the assembly the same as if it had been interupted by an adjournment.

10. If the motion is decided in the negative it is a discharge of the orders so far as they interfered with the consideration of the subject then pending.

11. Orders of the day unless proceeded in and disposed of on the day assigned, fall, of course, and must be renewed for some other day, or they will be thereby no longer pending.

12. Where a call for the orders of the day is voted down, the orders of the day stand postponed indefinitely and other business prevails.

13. Where a call for the order of the day prevails all other business is suspended.

14. A call for the order of the day is not debatable and is not subject to amendment.

### INCIDENTAL QUESTIONS.

#### 1. *Questions of Order.*

1. It is the duty of the presiding officer to enforce the rules and order of the assembly without question, debate or delay.

2. It is the right of every member taking notice of the breach of a rule to insist upon the enforcement of it.

3. Questions frequently arise as to there being a breach of order in a violation of rules; these are called questions of order.

4. When a question of order arises in the course of any other proceeding, it supersedes the further consideration of the subject out of which it arises until the question of order is disposed of.

5. When a question of order is settled the original motion or proceeding revives and resumes its former position unless it has been disposed of by the question of order.

6. When a question of order is raised by a member it is not stated from the chair and decided by the assembly, but it is stated by the member raising it, and decided in the

first instance by the presiding officer without debate.

7. The presiding officer may before giving his decision on a question of order raised invite the opinion and advice of experienced members present on the subject.

8. Where a decision of the presiding officer on a question of order is not satisfactory, any one member may object to it and have the question decided by the assembly, called an appeal from the decision of the chair.

9. On appeal from a decision of the chair on a question of order, the presiding officer is allowed to take part in the debate, from his place in the chair.

10. Questions of order are those raised by any member as to a breach of any rule. It is the privilege of any member to raise questions of order.

## 2. *Reading Papers.*

1. Reading of papers brought before an assembly may be called for by any member.

2. Where papers are brought before the assembly for action, every member has a right to have them read once at the table before he can be compelled to vote on them.

3. But where a member desires the reading of a paper or other matter, not before

the assembly for action, or to read his own speech, printed or in writing, if objection is made, the reading can not proceed without leave of the assembly.

4. Where in the course of debate or other proceeding the reading of a paper is called for, and a question being made as to its being read, this question is incidental to the former, and must be first decided.

### 3. *Withdrawal of a Motion.*

1. A motion regularly made and stated from the chair, or proposition regularly pending, is in possession of the assembly and can not be withdrawn, except by leave or vote of the assembly.

2. Where leave is granted to withdraw a motion, the withdrawing of the same takes with it all pending motions directly relating to it.

3. A motion for leave to withdraw a motion is not debatable.

### 4. *Suspension of a Rule.*

1. The suspension of a rule, where special rules are existing, may be ordered by vote of the assembly to consider a proposition which would not otherwise be in order.

### 5. *Amendment to an Amendment.*

2. Where a motion to amend an amend-

ment is made, such motion must be first put; if carried in the affirmative, the question then recurs on the amendment as amended.

3. The motion to amend an amendment is incidental to the latter and supersedes it for the time being.

4. It is proper to move to amend a proposed amendment, but a vote to further amend it can not be entertained.

## OF RECONSIDERATION.

1. In the absence of any express rule, a principal question disposed of by vote of the assembly, either in the affirmative or negative, may be reconsidered by vote of the majority, on motion, as in other cases.

2. A motion to reconsider being decided in the negative, it is a final disposition of the question and can not be again moved.

3. In the absence of any special rule of the assembly, a motion to reconsider may be made by any member, without reference to whether he voted in the affirmative or negat ve on the original question.

4. Where a motion to reconsider prevails, the question pending will be on the original proposition, the same as it stood before any vote thereon was taken, and in like manner again open to debate.

5. A motion to reconsider applies in general to a principal question, or some material motion. It does not apply to incidental motions, and the like.

## Of Committees.

### DIFFERENT KINDS OF COMMITTEES.

1. The committees in deliberative assemblies are: 1. Standing committees. 2. Select committees. 3. Committee of the whole.

### STANDING AND SELECT COMMITTEES.

2. Standing committees are those appointed to stand during the term of the assembly.

3. Select committees are those appointed to consider a particular subject.

4. Committee of the whole is a committee comprised of all the members of the assembly, to consider any subject referred to them.

5. Standing and select committees in the absence of any express rule or vote of the assembly are appointed by the presiding officer.

6. The first person named on a committee is considered the chairman, but in the absence of any rule or custom to the contrary

the committee may appoint one of their number as chairman.

7. It is the duty of a committee to report their opinion on the merits of the questions referred to them, either for or against them, but they may forbear an opinion and ask to be discharged from further consideration of the subject.

8. A committee can not properly in their report recommend dilatory action, as that the subject be laid on the table, postponed, referred to some other committee, and the like.

9. When a report of a committee is made, it is customary for the assembly to receive the same without any further vote thereon.

10. When the report of a select committee is received the committee are discharged without any action of the assembly.

11. After a report of the committee is received, the question recurs on its adoption, and this without any formal action to that end.

12. After a report is adopted the recommendation of the committee becomes the sense of the assembly.

### COMMITTEE OF THE WHOLE.

1. A committee of the whole is comprised of all the members of the assembly, organized as a committee.

2. In committee of the whole the strict rules of order governing the assembly itself in the dispatch of business, are dispensed with, and only general necessary rules are observed.

3. If a motion to go into the committee of the whole prevails, it is customary for the presiding officer of the assembly to designate some member to act as chairman, but in the absence of any special rule to the contrary the committee may disregard such appointment and select their own chairman.

4. In organizing the committee of the whole nothing further is necessary than the selection of a chairman. The selection of a clerk is a matter of discretion of the committee.

5. To constitute a committee of the whole for business a quorum or majority of the members of the assembly should be present.

6. Where there is not a quorum present the committee should rise and report the fact to the assembly for its action.

7. Where a proposition referred to the committee of the whole consists of several questions or progressions, the same should be considered separately, beginning with the first in number. After reading each it is open to debate.

8. In committee of the whole, privileged,

subsidiary, and incidental questions of a dilatory character are, in general, not recognized.

9. The following general rules are laid down. 1. The previous question can not be moved in committee of the whole; 2. The committee can not allow other committees to adjourn to some time and place; 3. Every member can speak as often as he can obtain the floor; 4. A committee of the whole can not refer a matter to another committee; 5. A committee of the whole has no authority to punish for a breach of order; matters of this kind should be referred to the assembly for action.

10. Debate on questions may be determined by a motion to close debate on the pending question.

11. As a general rule dilatory motions are not practicable in a committee of the whole.

12. When a committee of the whole desire to terminate their session it is done on motion that the committee rise and report progress.

13. No formal record of the proceedings of the committee of the whole is required to be kept. It is sufficient to preserve a brief memorandum.

## Appeals.

1. If the decision of a presiding officer on a question raised is not satisfactory, any member may except to it and demand that it be decided by the assembly—called an appeal from the decision of the chair.

2. On appeal the question is stated by the presiding officer, thus: "Shall the decision of the chair stand as the decision of the assembly," or "as the decision of the house?"

3. On appeal from the decision of the chair the question is open to debate and is decided by the assembly the same as any other question.

4. An appeal from a decision of the presiding officer may be taken at any time and moved even while another member has the floor.

5. An appeal may be withdrawn by the member moving it.

6. An appeal may be laid upon the table in the manner of other questions, which is considered a final disposition of the subject.

7. Laying an appeal upon the table has been adopted as a mode of disposing of the subject without expressing an opinion upon it.

## DEBATE.

1. When any member desires to speak he is to stand up in his place and address himself to the speaker.

2. When a member stands up to speak, no question as a general rule is to be put to the assembly while he is speaking, but he is to be heard to the end of his remarks, unless the assembly overrule for some breach of order.

3. Where two members rise to address the presiding officer at the same time, the member whose voice is first heard should be accorded the floor.

4. If two or more members rise to speak at the same time, the presiding officer determines who was first up, subject to appeal, however, in the absence of any special rule to the contrary.

5. Where a decision of the chair in according the floor to a member in case two or more rise at the same time is called in question, the question may be decided by taking the sense of the assembly thereon by appeal, as in other cases.

6. In taking the sense of the assembly in the case aforesaid, the question should be first taken on the name of the member announced by the presiding officer; if this is

lost, then it should be taken upon the member next in order claiming the floor.

7. A member obtaining the floor for a particular purpose, as in case of the chairman of a committee for the purpose of making a report, is not entitled to occupy the floor for any other purpose except by leave of the assembly.

8. Before there can be any debate in a deliberative assembly, there must be some question properly pending, which is debatable.

9. A member who has the floor for any purpose, must yield the same to the presiding officer when he rises to give information or state a point of order.

10. When a member who has the floor in debate is called to order, he must cease speaking and yield the floor until the question of order is decided.

11. When a member who has the floor yields it to another, although temporarily with the understanding between them that he may resume it presently, he loses his right to resume it again, except by leave of the assembly.

12. When a member in debate desires the reading of papers, he should send them to the clerk or secretary to be read. It is not

strictly in order for a member to read them himself from his place on the floor.

13. It is a general rule that no member can speak more than once on the same proposition, but where amendments are proposed he may speak to each amendment. But a member may be permitted to speak again to clear a matter of fact, or merely explain himself in some material part of his speech.

14. The presiding officer may have a right to speak of matters of order and be first heard, but not otherwise, except by leave of the assembly.

15. The presiding officer being a member of the assembly, may call some member to the chair, and on resuming his place on the floor may speak to a pending question the same as other members.

16. No member is to speak impertinently, tediously, or depart from the question pending.

17. Members are not allowed in debate to reflect on any prior determination of the assembly, unless he intends to conclude with a motion to rescind it.

18. While a proposition under consideration is undetermined, although it has been reported by a committee, reflections on it are no reflections on the assembly.

19. No member in speaking is to mention another member then present by his name.

20. No member is to disturb another in his speech by hissing, coughing, or other like conduct.

21. In case of disorder, if repeated calls do not produce order, the presiding officer may call by his name any member obstinately persisting in irregularity.

22. Disorderly words on the part of a member are not to be noticed until he has finished his speech; then the person objecting to them and desiring them to be taken down by the clerk must repeat them. The presiding officer may direct the clerk to take them down in his minutes, but if he thinks them not disorderly he may delay the direction.

23. After disorderly words are taken down by the clerk, the matter is open to the action of the assembly.

24. When a member has spoken, or other business intervened after disorderly or offensive words spoken, such words cannot then be taken notice of for censure.

25. Disorderly words spoken in a committee must be written down as in the assembly, but the committee can only report them to the assembly for action.

It is a breach of order in debate in legislative assemblies to notice what has been said on the same subject in the other house, and the particular votes and majorities in the other.

Neither house in legislative assemblies can exercise any authority over a member or officer of the other, but should complain to the house of which he is a member or officer.

Penalty for misconduct of a member may be by repremanding, exclusion from the assembly, a prohibition to vote or speak for a specified time, or expulsion.

## Use of the Gavel.

One rap of the gavel only should be given by the presiding officer in calling the assembly to order.

One rap of the gavel is proper in announcing that any particular order of business is closed.

One rap of the gavel may be given in commanding the attention of members for any purpose.

One rap of the gavel should be given when declaring the assembly adjourned.

# INDEX.

|  | Page |
|---|---|
| ADJOURNMENT—*See Motion to Adjourn.* | |
| General rules concerning | 136 |

**AMENDMENT.**
Various modes of.................................................. 53, 59
Filling blanks...................................................... 53, 134
Striking out......................................................... 55, 134
Striking out and inserting................................... 56, 135
Division of a proposition..................................... 56, 135
Amendment to an amendment............................ 59
Amendment of an amendment is an incidental
    question........................................................... 61
General rules concerning..................................... 133
By inserting......................................................... 134

**AMENDMENT BY INSERTING.**
Mode of proceeding............................................. 55
General rules concerning............................ 55, 56, 134

**AMENDMENT TO AN AMENDMENT.**
General rules concerning................................... 59, 142
Is an incidental question..................................... 61
Proceeding in case of.......................................... 62
May be debated.................................................. 93

**APPEALS.**
General rules concerning................................... 82, 143
From decision of presiding officer.................... 82, 83
Mode of taking.................................................. 83
Question open to debate.................................. 83, 143
Mode of putting question.......................... 143, 143
May be taken at any time................................ 143
May be taken while another member has the floor.. 143
May be withdrawn............................................ 143
May be laid on the table.................................. 143

**ASSISTANT SECRETARY.**
At public meetings............................................ 38

   Page

**BARON.**
   Is of Saxon origin................................................................ 16

**BOARD OF SUPERVISORS**—*See County Boards.*

**BREACH OF ORDER**—*See Debate.*
   To speak of proceedings in the other house in debate................................................................ 90

**BRITISH LEGISLATURE.**
   Is composed of king, or queen, lords and commons ........................................................11, 13

**BRITISH PARLIAMENT.** *See Legislation in Parliament.*
   History of................................................................ 11
   Originally consisted of the house of lords................ 11
   Enacting clause in bills................................ 96, 101
   Peculiarities of legislation in........................ 110

**CASTING VOTE.**
   Rules concerning.................................... 95, 96

**CHAIRMAN.**
   Must be one in deliberative assembly............ 26, 30
   Presiding officer when so called........................ 35
   Chairman of committee call meeting to order........ 35
   Choosing at organization of public meeting............ 36
   Opening address of........................................ 36
   Proceeding by in organizing public meeting............ 37
   When should state object of the meeting........ 37, 38
   Should announce when meeting is fully organized... 40
   Mode of proceeding in putting motions and taking question................................................ 43, 46
   Of standing and select committees........................ 69
   Of committee of the whole.................... 74, 75, 76
   Appeal from decisions of................................ 82
   Privileges and duties of in debate........ 86, 88, 89
   Presides in deliberative assembly...................... 122

**CHAIRMAN OF COMMITTEE.**
   When should call meeting to order.................... 35

**CITY COUNCILS.**
   Parliamentary law applicable............................ 34

**CLERK**—*See Recording Officer.*
   Is recording officer in deliberative assembly.... 31, 122

## INDEX.

Page

**COMMITTEE.**
Motion to refer to proper motion to suppress proposition.................................................................. 48
Prepare and report business............................................ 41
General rules concerning........................68, 73, 144, 148
Committees are of three kinds..................................... 68
Select committees ............................................................. 68
Standing committees........................................................ 68
Committee of the whole.................................................. 68
Disorderly words in, proceeding.................................. 90

**COMMITTEES.** *See Committee.*
General rules concerning....................................... 144, 148
Different kinds of............................................................ 144
Standing and select......................................................... 144
Committee of the whole........................................ 145, 148

**COMMITTEE OF THE WHOLE.**
Of whom comprised.......................................................... 68
Power and duties of................................................... 73, 82
Assembly may resolve itself into................................. 74
Mode of proceeding.................................................. 74, 78
Chairman, how appointed............................................... 75
Clerk of.............................................................................. 75
Meetings of....................................................................... 76
Quorum............................................................................... 76
Meeting of, how adjourn................................................ 79
No record of proceedings required............................. 80
Report of........................................................................... 81
Disorderly words in, proceeding................................. 90
General rules concerning........................................ 145, 148

**COUNTY BOARDS.**
When parliamentary law applicable.............................. 84

**DEBATE.**
General rules concerning.................... 83, 92, 149, 153
Rule when member desires to speak............................. 84
Where two or more rise at same time presiding officer decides................................................................. 84
Decision may be appealed from..................................... 85
Member to speak but once on same question............ 85
Exception to foregoing.................................................... 85
When presiding officer may speak................................ 86
Member not to depart from question nor speak impertinently............................................................ 86, 87
Not to mention another member by name................. 87
Members not to disturb another in his speech......... 87

                                                                Page
DEBATE—*Continued*.
  When presiding officer may call member by name.... 88
  Disorderly words, proceeding on............................ 88, 89
  Breach of order to mention proceedings in the
    other house................................................................ 90
  Member should not be present in debate concern-
    ing himself................................................................ 91
  Manner of obtaining the floor.................................... 124

DECISION—*See Appeals*.
  Of presiding officer appeal from............................ 82, 85

DELIBERATIVE ASSEMBLIES.
  Remarks concerning................................................ 22, 26
  Definition of............................................................ 22
  Of the word assembly.............................................. 22
  Difference between deliberative assembly and ex-
    ecutive board........................................................... 22
  When rules of parliamentary law apply.................... 23
  May be assembly of the people................................ 23
  May be meeting of limited or select number of
    citizens..................................................................... 23
  Neglect, or departure from rules of proceeding........ 24
  Rules are protection to minorities......................... 24, 25
  Essentials which mark deliberative assemblies......... 26
  Organization consists in election of officers............. 26
  Classification of officers.......................................... 26
  General rules concerning......................................... 121
  Officers in................................................................ 122

DEPORTMENT OF MEMBERS.
  General rules concerning..................................... 106, 110
  Nicknames should be avoided.................................. 108

DISORDERLY WORDS.
  In debate, proceeding on...................................... 88, 89
  In committee, proceeding on.................................... 90

DIVISION OF A PROPOSITION.
  Mode of proceeding................................................ 56
  General remarks concerning........................... 56, 59, 135

DIVISION OF THE HOUSE.
  When may be called for........................................... 125
  Manner of taking..................................................... 125
  When must be called for.......................................... 126

DOOR KEEPER.
  In deliberative assemblies........................................ 26

INDEX.                                                159

|                                                           | Page |

EARL.
Is of Saxon origin........................................................ 16

ENACTING CLAUSE.
History of.................................................................. 96

ENACTING WORDS—*See Enacting Clause.*
Origin of the term....................................................... 97

EXECUTIVE BOARD.
What constitutes......................................................... 22
Rules for government of.............................................. 22

FEUDAL SYSTEM.
House of Lords is outgrowth of................................... 12

FILLING BLANKS.
Mode of proceeding in.......................................... 53, 55
General rules concerning............................................ 134

FREE MASONS—*See Free Masonry.*
Conduct proceedings under parliamentary law........... 34
Parliamentary law applicable..................................... 115
Origin and history of................................................. 115

FREE MASONRY—*See Masonic Order, Masonic Lodges.*
Origin and history of........................................ 115, 116
When interdicted in England..................................... 116
Odd Fellows in imitation of....................................... 116

GAVEL—*See Use of the Gavel.*

GENERAL RULES.
Summary of............................................................... 121
In motions and manner of proceeding.............. 128, 130

HOUSE OF COMMONS.
Origin of................................................................ 12, 13
Called lower house of parliament................................ 13
Manner of voting in......................................... 110, 111

HOUSE OF LORDS.
Means the same thing as peers.................................... 11
Is the second of three bodies composing legislature.... 11
Origin of..................................................................... 11
Origin involved in obscurity....................................... 11
Is of older date than Norman conquest....................... 12
Great council of early English chroniclers................. 12

HOUSE OF LORDS—*Continued.*               **Page**
  Known as upper house of parliament ............... 13
  Possesses judicial authority ............................. 14
  Trying cases of impeachment and its own members on indictment ............................................. 14
  Points in which it differs from lower house of parliament ......................................................... 14
  Lord Chancellor sits as speaker .......................... 14
  Sovereign sits in to open or dissolve parliament ... 14
  When the commons are summoned ..................... 14
  Bills affecting dignity of peerage must originate in ................................................................. 14, 15
  Members have right of voting by proxy ............... 15
  Peers have privilege of dissent from any measure .. 15
  Peers of England have seats and votes in ............ 17
  And so of Great Britain and United Kingdom ...... 17
  Manner of voting in ..................................... 110, 111

INCIDENTAL QUESTIONS.
  Arise out of other questions ............................ 61, 128
  Decided before those which give rise to them .... 61, 128
  What are ............................................. 61, 126, 127, 128
  In general not debatable .................................... 93
  General rules concerning ................................... 140

INDEFINITE POSTPONEMENT.
  Subsidiary motion to suppress proposition ........... 48
  Is decided without debate .................................. 50
  Removes question from before assembly ............. 50
  Motion to postpone beyond session .................... 50
  Not debatable .................................................... 93

JUDICIAL AUTHORITY.
  House of Lords possesses .................................. 14

LANGUAGE OF PARLIAMENTARY LAW.
  General rules to be observed ....................... 112, 115
  Slang phrases to be avoided ............................. 113
  What are proper terms to be used ............... 113, 114

LEGISLATION IN PARLIAMENT.
  Peculiarities of ........................................... 110, 111
  Bills, how engrossed ......................................... 110
  When bills amended, rider ................................ 110
  How members vote in house of commons ........... 110
  How members vote in house of peers ................. 110
  The king's answer to bills ................................. 110
  When speaker is so called ................................ 110
  Mode of taking vote in house of commons .......... 111

## LIE ON THE TABLE.
A subsidiary motion to suppress proposition............ 48
Proposition laid on the table can not be considered without vote to take it up................................... 50
When laid on the table may be taken up by vote of assembly ............................................................ 50
Motion to take from the table not a privileged motion................................................................... 51
Not recognized in some States of the Union......... 51, 52
Equivalent motion is motion to postpone for the present ............................................................... 52
Definition and use of ............................................ 62
Takes precedence of other subsidiary motions......... 63
Not debatable....................................................... 92
When qualified, is debatable.................................. 93
General rules concerning...................................... 130

## LIEUTENANT-GOVERNOR.
Has casting vote.................................................. 95

## LORD CHANCELLOR.
Sits as speaker in house of Lords.......................... 14

## MAIN QUESTION.
Under the previous question ................................ 49

## MAJORITY.
Voice of in either house binds the whole................ 13
Neglect or departure from rules throws power into hands of............................................................. 24
Rules are a check on the action of........................ 24

## MANNER OF PROCEEDING—*See Motions.*
General rules concerning.................................. 128, 143

## MANNER OF PRESENTING BUSINESS.
Right of members to present propositions............. 41
By motion or resolution...................................... 41
By report of committee....................................... 41
General rules concerning ............................... 122, 126

## MASONIC LODGES.
Parliamentary law in .......................................... 115
Authority of master............................................. 117
No privileged questions in ................................... 118
No motion to adjourn in ...................................... 118
What questions excluded..................................... 118
Conduct proceedings in manner of deliberative assemblies....................................................... 116

|  | Page |
|---|---|
| **MASONIC ORDER**—*See Masonic Lodges.* | |
| Parliamentary law in | 115 |
| **MASS MEETING.** | |
| What constitutes | 23 |
| **MAYOR OF CITY.** | |
| When should call public meeting to order | 35 |
| **MEMORIAL.** | |
| Definition of | 123 |
| Differs from petition | 123 |
| Presentation of | 123 |
| **MINORITY.** | |
| Rules are a protection to | 25 |
| **MODERATOR.** | |
| Presiding officer in religious meetings and town meetings | 30 |
| **MOTION**—*See Motions in General, Motion to Commit.* | |
| Business presented by | 41, 122 |
| Is a proposition of a member | 42, 123 |
| Seconded by one member | 42 |
| Presumed to be seconded | 42, 129 |
| Seconding a matter of form | 43 |
| Necessary for action on questions | 43 |
| Manner of putting by chairman | 43, 44 |
| When seconded, becomes property of the assembly | 44 |
| Can not be withdrawn except by leave | 44, 125 |
| Vote on | 45 |
| Division on vote may be called for | 45 |
| Proceeding when division called for | 46 |
| When tellers may be appointed | 46 |
| After previous question, how disposed of | 49 |
| To postpone or lie on the table | 50 |
| To postpone beyond session is indefinite postponement | 50 |
| Motion to take from the table not a privileged motion | 51 |
| To amend, different modes of | 53 |
| To adjourn takes place of other motions | 60 |
| Leave to withdraw is an incidental question | 61 |
| Withdrawal of | 61 |
| To postpone | 63 |
| To commit | 63 |
| To amend | 64 |

|  | Page |
|---|---|
| **MOTION**—*Continued.* | |
| Order of standing | 64 |
| Example of, succession of | 64 |
| To adjourn not debatable | 92 |
| To lie on the table not debatable | 92 |
| For previous question not debatable | 93 |
| For indefinite postponement not debatable | 93 |
| For reading papers not debatable | 93 |
| To take up particular subject not debatable | 93 |
| Can not be made until member has the floor | 124 |
| Not before assembly until stated | 124 |
| Not before assembly until read | 125 |
| Difference between motion and question | 126 |
| Required to be seconded | 128 |
| Mode of seconding | 129 |
| When member cannot occupy the floor for two motions | 129 |
| To suppress a proposition | 129 |
| **MOTIONS IN GENERAL.** | |
| When put to the assembly | 47 |
| Subsidiary motions | 47, 48, 126, 127 |
| Previous question | 48 |
| To lie on the table | 48 |
| Indefinite postponement | 48 |
| Postponement to future time | 48 |
| To refer to committee | 48 |
| To amend | 48 |
| Different kinds of motions | 126 |
| Principal motion presumed to be always pending | 126 |
| **MOTION TO ADJOURN.** | |
| Not debatable | 92 |
| **MOTION TO AMEND.** | |
| Nature of amendments | 53 |
| Filling blanks | 53, 55 |
| Striking out | 55 |
| Striking out and inserting | 56 |
| Division of a proposition | 56, 59 |
| Amendment to an amendment | 59 |
| Order and standing of | 64 |
| **MOTION TO COMMIT.** | |
| Use and nature of this motion | 52, 53 |
| Motion to refer to select and standing committee may be pending at the same time | 52 |
| Motion to refer to standing committe takes precedence of motion to refer to select committee | 52 |

## MOTION TO COMMIT—*Continued*.

Page

Motion to refer to standing committee should be first put; part or whole of subject may be referred.................................................... 52
Portions may be referred to different committees..... 52
After motion to commit, motion to amend not in order................................................................. 52
When motion to commit may be amended by substituting another committee................................. 52
Motion to refer to select committee may be amended as to number of committee................................ 53
On motion to commit the committee may be instructed................................................................ 53
If motion to commit is carried, subject is removed from the assembly........................................... 53
How may be amended................................................... 63
Takes precedence of motion to amend........................ 64
General rules concerning............................................. 132

## MOTION TO POSTPONE.

Is proper motion to consider proposition at future time.................................................................. 50
Question postponed to time fixed when time arrives consideration is in order.......................... 50
Is either indefinite or to time certain........................... 63
When treated like filling blanks.................................... 63
For indefinite postponement not debatable................ 93
To time certain is debatable........................................ 93

## ODD FELLOWS.

Proceedings conducted under parliamentary law..... 34
Had its rise in England following masonry................ 116
In imitation of masonry............................................... 116
Lodges, parliamentary law in...................................... 116

## OFFICERS.

In deliberative assemblies................................... 26, 122
Presiding officer........................................................... 27
Recording officer......................................................... 31
At public meetings....................................................... 35

## ORDERS OF THE DAY.

Come thirdly in succession under privileged questions.................................................................. 61
Why so called............................................................... 61
General rules concerning.................................... 138, 140

|                                          | Page |
|---|---|
|                                          |      |

**ORGANIZATION OF PUBLIC MEETINGS.**
Mode of organizing........................................... 35, 40
Choose presiding officer and secretary................ 34
Meeting called to order..................................... 35
Mode of calling meeting to order....................... 36
Mode of choosing officers................................. 36, 37
Address of presiding officer, form of..............36, note.
Stating object of meeting.................................. 37, 38
Delegate convention, mode of proceeding.......... 38, 39
Temporary organization.................................... 35, 39
Completion of organization............................... 40

**PARLIAMENTARY LAW.**
Origin and use of.............................................. 21, 22
Consists of rules recognized in deliberative assemblies..................................................... 21
Why so called................................................... 21
Adopted in legislative assemblies....................... 21
Standard of....................................................... 21, 22
Applicable to town meetings.............................. 33
When applicable to county board....................... 34
Applicable to city and town councils.................. 34
Societies and secret orders............................... 34, 115
General rules concerning................................... 121

**PARLIAMENT**—*See British Parliament.*

**PEERAGE.**
Of Great Britain and Ireland, classification of...... 16
Spiritual peers, who are.................................... 17
In house of Lords all peers of England have seats and votes................................................. 17

**PEERS**—*See House of Lords.*
Various classes and rank of............................... 15
Of Scotland and Ireland..................................... 18
Minors and Insane disqualified.......................... 19

**PETITION.**
Definition of..................................................... 123
Presentation of................................................ 123
Difference from memorial.................................. 123

**POSTPONEMENT**—*See Indefinite Postponement—Motion to Postpone.*
General rules concerning................................... 132

**POSTPONEMENT TO FUTURE TIME.**
A subsidiary motion to suppress proposition...... 48

|  | Page |
|---|---|
| **PREAMBLE.** | |
| Part of bill | 97 |
| **PRESIDENT**—*See Chairman.* | |
| In deliberative assembly | 29, 30, 122 |
| Presiding officer so called in large meetings | 35 |
| **PRINCIPAL MOTION.** | |
| Definition of | 127 |
| **PRESIDING OFFICER**—*See Chairman, President, Speaker.* | |
| Must be one in deliberative assembly | 26 |
| General duties of | 27, 30 |
| To open sessions of the assembly | 27 |
| Announce business before the assembly | 27 |
| Submit motions and propositions | 27 |
| Put to vote questions | 27 |
| Name members entitled to the floor in debate | 27 |
| Restrain members and keep order | 27, 28 |
| To receive messages and communications | 28 |
| Authenticate acts, orders and proceedings | 28 |
| Decide points of order | 28 |
| Name members to serve on committees | 29 |
| Represent and stand for the assembly | 29 |
| Should rise to put a motion | 29, 125 |
| Is styled president or chairman | 29, 30 |
| In some instances styled moderator | 30 |
| In popular branch of legislative assemblies styled speaker | 30 |
| To announce results of votes or action of the assembly | 32 |
| Appeal from decision of | 82 |
| When decision final | 125 |
| **PREVIOUS QUESTION.** | |
| Is a subsidiary question | 48 |
| A subsidiary motion to suppress proposition | 48 |
| Practice and proceedings under | 49 |
| Stands in equal degree with other motions, except to lie on the table | 63 |
| Not debatable | 93 |
| General rules concerning | 131 |
| **PRIVILEGED QUESTIONS** | |
| What are | 60, 126, 127, 128 |
| Orders of the day are | 61 |
| Are independent questions | 128 |
| Have no reference to main question | 128 |

# INDEX.

**PRIVILEDGED QUESTIONS—**Continued.*

| | Page |
|---|---|
| May be pending with main question | 1, 8 |
| General rules concerning | 136 |

**PROTEST.**
Meaning of in British parliament........................ 15

**PUBLIC MEETINGS.**
General remarks concerning........................ 33, 34
Rules of parliamentary law apply........................ 33
County boards when parliamentary law applicable... 33
In towns under township organization in New England and some other States........................ 34
City and town councils parliamentary law applicable........................ 34
Societies and secret orders parliamentary law applicable........................ 34
Convening public meetings........................ 34
Organization of........................ 35, 40
Choose presiding officer and secretary........................ 85

**QUESTIONS.**
Order and succession of........................ 59
Privileged questions........................ 60
Of privilege........................ 60
Incidental........................ 61

**QUESTIONS NOT DEBATABLE.**
What questions are not debatable........................ 92, 95

**QUESTIONS OF ORDER.**
Come under head of incidental questions........................ 61
What are........................ 61
General rules concerning........................ 140

**QUESTIONS OF PRIVILEGE.**
Order and definition of........................ 60
In general not debatable........................ 93
General rules concerning........................ 137

**QUORUM.**
In committee of the whole........................ 76
General rules concerning........................ 122
What constitutes........................ 122
Business cannot proceed without........................ 122
Number may be fixed by rules........................ 122
All questions determined by majority of........................ 122

**READING PAPERS.**  Page
  Motions for.............................................................. 61
  Come under head of incidental questions................ 61
  May be called for by any member............................ 61
  Motion for not debatable.......................................... 93
  General rules concerning........................................ 141

**RECONSIDERATION.**
  Vote of assembly may be reconsidered.................... 65
  Made in same manner as other motions.................. 65
  Is of American origin................................................ 65
  Once decided is final................................................ 66
  Motion may be made by any member...................... 66
  Proceedings under.................................................... 65
  Whole subject open for debate................................ 67
  General rules concerning........................................ 143

**RECORDING OFFICER.**
  In deliberative assembly.......................................... 31
  Election and duties of......................................... 31, 33
  Is styled secretary or clerk...................................... 31
  In large bodies usually styled secretary.................. 31
  Duty to make entry of proceedings.......................... 31
  Read all papers coming before the assembly.......... 31
  Call the roll of members.......................................... 32
  Notify committees of their appointment.................. 32
  Authenticate proceedings in connection with president.................................................................. 32
  Charged with custody of papers and journals.......... 32
  Guided by presiding officer in recording proceedings..................................................................... 32
  Extent under control of presiding officer................ 32
  Shall stand while reading papers or calling the assembly..................................................................... 33

**REPORT OF COMMITTEE.**
  Manner of making.................................................... 69
  Proceeding on making.............................................. 72

**RESOLUTION.**
  Business presented by.............................................. 41
  Is a proposition in writing...................................... 123
  When offered motion not necessary........................ 124
  Motion implied........................................................ 124

**SECRETARY**—*See Recording Officer.*
  Must be one in deliberative assembly................26, 122
  Is the recording officer in deliberative assembly...... 31

|  | Page |
|---|---|
| **SECRETARY**—*Continued.* | |
| Election of at public meeting | 37 |
| When to count votes of the assembly | 46 |
| **SELECT COMMITTEE**—*See Committee.* | |
| On motion to refer to standing and select committee, former first put | 52 |
| Motion to refer to select committee amended by changing number | 53 |
| Are appointed for particular subject | 68 |
| By whom appointed | 68 |
| Who chairman of | 69 |
| Manner of making report | 69 |
| Duties of | 71 |
| Proceeding on making report | 72 |
| Disorderly words in, proceeding | 90 |
| **SERGEANT-AT-ARMS.** | |
| In deliberative assembly | 26 |
| **SOCIETIES AND SECRET ORDERS.** | |
| In general conducted under parliamentary law | 84 |
| Parliamentary law in | 115 |
| **SPEAKER.** | |
| Presiding officer in legislative assemblies so called | 30 |
| Origin of and why so called | 30, 111 |
| When appoints tellers | 111 |
| **SPIRITUAL PEERS**—*See Peers.* | |
| Of whom they consist | 17 |
| **STANDING COMMITTEES**—*See Committee.* | |
| When subjects should be referred to | 52 |
| Motion to refer to standing and select, former first put | 52 |
| Purposes of | 68 |
| By whom appointed | 68 |
| Who chairman of | 69 |
| Manner of making report | 69 |
| Duties of | 71 |
| Proceeding on making report | 72 |
| Disorderly words in, proceeding | 90 |
| **STRIKING OUT.** | |
| Mode of proceeding on motion | 55 |
| General rules concerning | 134 |

## INDEX.

**STRIKING OUT AND INSERTING.**                              Page
  Mode of proceeding on motion .................................. 56
  Motion may be divided ............................................ 56
  General rules concerning ........................................ 135

**STYLE.**
  Of laws ........................................................ 98, 99, 100

**STYLE OF LAWS**—*See Style.*

**SUBSIDIARY MOTION.**
  Order and description of ....................................... 47, 48
  Those in common use .................................. 62, 126, 127
  Nature of ................................................................ 127
  General rules concerning ................................... 129, 136

**SUBSIDIARY QUESTIONS**—*See Subsidiary Motion.*
  Lie on the table .................................................... 62
  Previous question ................................................ 63
  Motion to commit ................................................ 63
  Motion to amend .................................................. 64
  Definition of ........................................................ 127

**SUSPENSION OF A RULE.**
  Is an incidental question ..................................... 61
  Object and purpose of ......................................... 62
  General rules concerning ..................................... 142

**TELLERS.**
  When to be appointed ..................................... 46, 47
  Mode of appointing .............................................. 125
  When demanded .................................................. 126

**TIE VOTE.**
  Proceedings in case of ......................................... 95

**TOWN COUNCILS.**
  Parliamentary law applicable ................................ 34

**TOWN MEETING.**
  Parliamentary law applicable ................................ 33

**USE OF THE GAVEL.**
  Had its origin in Masonic lodges ........................ 101
  Called common gavel or stone hammer ............ 102
  An emblem of authority ...................................... 102
  Number of raps in using ............................... 102, 103
  In case of noise or confusion ............................ 104

Page

**USE OF THE GAVEL—*Continued*.**
In calling assembly to order.............................. 103, 105
Should not be held constantly in hand..................... 105
General rules concerning ........................................ 153

**VICE-PRESIDENT.**
In deliberative assemblies........................................ 26
At public meetings .................................................. 38
Has casting vote....................................................... 95

**WITHDRAWAL OF MOTION.**
Is allowed on leave................................................. 61
General rules concerning....................................... 142

www.ingramcontent.com/pod-product-compliance
Lightning Source LLC
Chambersburg PA
CBHW022115160426
43197CB00009B/1042